Food for thought

Joan Morecroft
Jonathan Smith

S · T · E · P

CAMBRIDGE
UNIVERSITY PRESS

S · T · E · P

5 16

DESIGN AND
TECHNOLOGY

Published by the Press Syndicate of the
University of Cambridge
The Pitt Building, Trumpington Street,
Cambridge CB2 1RP
10 Stamford Road, Oakleigh,
Melbourne 3166, Australia

© Cambridge University Press 1993

First published 1993

In association with Staffordshire County Council

Designed and produced by Gecko Limited,
Bicester, Oxon

Printed in Great Britain at the University Press,
Cambridge

A catalogue record for this book is available from
the British Library

Library of Congress data applied for

ISBN 0 521 40636 6 ✓

Cover illustration by Michaela Blunden

Acknowledgements

The STEP team and publishers would sincerely like
to thank the following for their help during the
research, writing and production of this book.

Christine Cross (Divisional Director, Technical
Services) at Tesco Stores Ltd for guidance on the
processes followed by Tesco in developing food
products.
Professor Bob McCormick (Open University) for
his invaluable discussions and advice on systems
thinking and representation.
Dr John Martin (Salford University) for his
suggestions on the systems and production
sections.
Gill Almond (Sandon High School) for her
contributions to the food production section.

Mike Davey (Thomas Alleyne's High School),
Joy Saunderson (Edgecliffe High School), Chris
Thompson (Cannock Chase High School) and John
Trevett (Cheadle High School) for their valued
comments on the 'Getting down to business'
section.
Sainsbury plc for information on critical path
analysis on page 29.

Also grateful thanks to other members of the STEP
team for their valuable contributions.

We would like to thank the following for their
permission to reproduce photographs.
Key: t=top, c=centre, b=bottom, l=left, r=right,
*=background.

Advertising Archives 7cl, 50tl, 50tr, 51c, 51bl, 51bc,
51cr, 52t, 52cl, 52c, 52cr, 54br, 55cl, 55c, 55cr, 55bl
Anthony Blake 58tl, 58tr
Cadbury Ltd 55br, 63, 67
Co-operative Wholesale Society Ltd 66
Counsel Ltd/Heinz 50b
CTC Tele Pictorials 55tl, 55tr
Economatics Education Ltd 83t
Ford 60cr
Robert Harding 5bl, 5bc, 49b, 50cl, 50cr, 60/1*,
68/9*, 81b, 88b, 88/9*, 93c
Image Bank 15tl, 28/9*, 32t, 49t, 53, 73t, 73c, 73br,
    81cl, 88tr
Kelloggs 7tr, 7cr
Leatherhead Food RA 25t
Mendle Ltd/Bel 89
Andry Montgomery Ltd 12/13*
Nestle UK Ltd 55bc
Robert Opie 11cl, 11cr, 11br
Science Photo Library 5br, 34bl, 49c, 59tl, 60cl,
    73bl, 88c, 93t, 93b
Sefton 60t, 60b
Visionbank 92cl

Bird's Eye Walls Ltd, Cadbury Ltd, Campden Food
& Drink RA, Co-operative Wholesale Society Ltd,
Didcot Community Education, The Environmental
Investigation Agency, Ford, Kellogg, Nestle UK Ltd
Porth Decorative Products, Swaddles Green Farm.

Staff at Tesco Bicester, in particular, and Abingdon
for assistance with location photographs.

Location and studio photography by Chris Coggins:
4/5*, 4, 5t, 6, 8, 11t, 11bl, 13, 14, 15tr, 15cl, 15cr,
15bl, 16br, 17, 19, 20, 22, 25bl, 25br, 26, 30, 31,
32b, 34c, 34r, 35, 36, 37, 39, 40, 42, 47, 48/9*, 51cl,
58b, 59tc, 59tr, 59b, 62, 65, 69, 70, 76, 78, 81t,
81cr, 83c, 83b, 91, 92bl, 92br, 94, 96.

Picture research by Jane Duff.

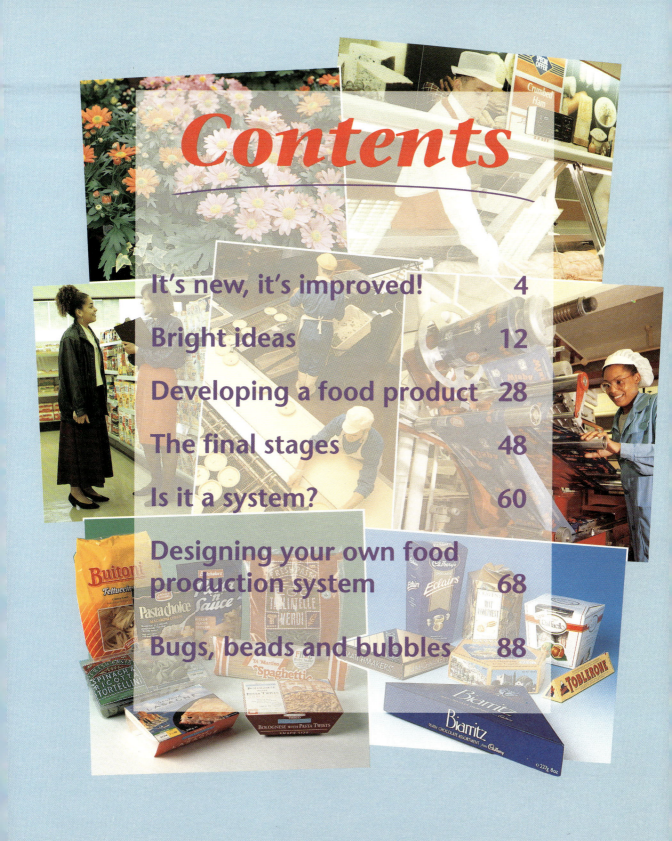

Contents

During recent years there has been a vast increase in the number and variety of ready-made food products available to the consumer. This has been brought about by many changes that have taken place in society: changes in people's lifestyle, changes in the buying power of the consumer, changes in structure of the retail trade and in food manufacture and distribution.

Vegetarian ▲

Other countries

Microwave

New ▼

Companies who produce food products, and those who sell them, need to be very competitive. To be successful they need to sell as much of their products as possible. Since we, as customers, can only consume so much food, this means they must continually attract more people to eat their products. Even then, customers like to change and try different foods. So it is important for companies to always be developing new food products.

What is a 'New' food product?

In many cases what appears as a new food product is not at all a new invention. Often it is a manufactured version of a food previously made individually, in the home, in a restaurant kitchen here or abroad, or by a specialist in a small shop.

Brainstorming ideas

Working in small groups, brainstorm a list of foods that are interesting, exciting or unusual that you have tasted in the past, perhaps at school or at home, and decide on their origin. When you were last on holiday did you discover a food that you really enjoyed? Was it something that others would like to eat?

Discuss your suggestions with your group and between you agree on one and give valid reasons why you think it would be a success. Think of a name which would attract people to buy it. Who do you think will buy it (that is your target group)?

Set your suggestions out like this.

Food Descriptor	Origin	Name	Target group

New or *improved?*

Somewhat different is the development of new or improved varieties within an existing range, such as different flavoured yogurts, a new soft cheese or mix of chopped vegetables and mayonnaise. Occasionally the food is prepared in different forms, as with frozen, chilled and dehydrated foods.

Really new or just improved?

Look at the items illustrated or, better still, make a collection of your own. Specifically take samples of those which claim to be 'NEW'. Have they been on the market previously? Are they really new or are they just altered or improved? Is it possible to determine how they are different so that the manufacturer is able to claim they are new?

Becoming a
household name

Manufacturers already involved in food production will
have existing products, facilities and expertise relating
to their current operations. The development of any
new product must fit into this existing structure and
not affect other operations. Therefore, food product
development tends to be evolutionary rather than
revolutionary. Companies usually stick with the type of
products they know well. It is also difficult for them to
expand into a market where they are not the recognised
supplier. For example, Kelloggs have been making
cornflakes for some 75 years! The product has
undergone little change and the packaging has always
remained familiar. Look at the examples and see if you
can pick out those things that have remained constant.

What do they sell?

Look at these names of companies.
Is it easy for you to identify them with
the products they sell? Make a list of
the products that each company
sells.

·DATA FILE·
Logos, signs and symbols
Lettering

Consumer *Choice*

Success sometimes lies in providing a new type of product. For instance, there has recently been the successful introduction of a whole range of 'healthy foods' on the basis of nutritional appeal, such as unsweetened fruit in natural juice, low fat dairy products, reduced calorie dishes, high fibre cereals and wholegrain bakery goods. Experience suggests that the consumer is influenced by the following factors.

- Is the product interesting? Will it appeal to the family?
- Does it look attractive?
- Does it look value for money?
- Is it good for you?
- Does it look tasty, fun to eat, etc?
- Is the portion size suitable?
- Is it easy/convenient to use?
- (after purchase) Was it thought to be good value for money?

Spotting influences on the consumer

Perhaps you could add to the list opposite. Discuss your ideas as a group. Which factors do you think have the greatest influence?

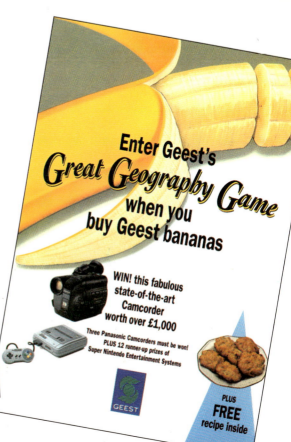

If the product is familiar it will be more easily accepted by consumers. This can be achieved through advance publicity and sales promotions. Products can also become more familiar from having been seen or experienced while on holiday or seen in a magazine.

SF

ONLY WHEN YOU BUY THIS PRODUCT

TESCO

20P OFF
NESTLÉ CINNAMON TOAST CRUNCH 400g

ONLY AT TESCO

Customer: This coupon can only be used in part payment against Nestlé ...on Toast Crunch 400g when purchased in any Tesco store (where stocked) ...sented with the product at the checkout. Only one coupon per purchase.

...PON VALID UNTIL 28th FEBRUARY 1993.

CPN1100 4/1-31/1

9904572560201

·DATA FILE·
Advertising
Nutritional guidelines
Presenting information

The product
development process

You can see a vast range of semi-prepared food items in stores nowadays, but do you know how much time and work has been going on behind the scenes to develop them?

To help us understand the development process, we are going to follow the type of process that takes place in large companies such as Tesco. It will answer questions such as these.

- How are new ideas produced?
- What is involved in taking an idea through to a place on a supermarket shelf?
- How can all the tasks that need to be done be coordinated for the launch day?

A company would employ a **development team** to design new food products. This team would have key members and others who are drawn in from time to time to help. The core team would include a product evaluation officer, a food technologist (Technical Department), the marketing manager and a buyer (Commercial Department). Others would include scientists, designers, quality assurance, barcoding, nutritionists and consumer law specialists.

Generation of ideas

↓

Concept screening

↓

Development

↓

First production run

↓

Advertising

↓

Product launch

One of the team's first jobs is to produce new ideas for food products. These food products may be aimed at filling a gap in the market or be suggested to tempt customers to try something new. Apart from staple foods that we buy regularly, the public likes to try new foods for a change. This means that some food products can be expected to have a definite life cycle. While they may be popular to start with, sales may start to dwindle after a while. Eventually they will be withdrawn from sale and replaced by something new. This is why companies need to develop new ideas.

As you will see there are different ways in which new ideas for foods can be produced. However, wherever the idea comes from, it will be necessary to do some market research to find out what the customers think.

Sterilised milk is being replaced by instant mix powders and UHT milk in cartons.

Liquid gravy browning has been largely replaced by gravy mix powders and gravy granules due to advances in the technology of drying and freeze-drying.

Do you know anyone who used to eat these?

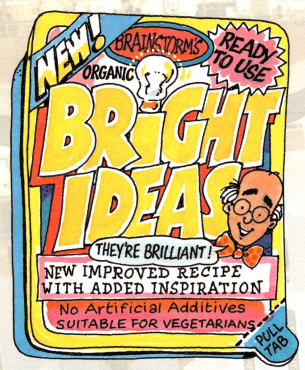

Product development begins with the generation of ideas. You must start with plenty of these in order to finish with a few excellent ones.

There are a number of ways to generate new ideas and it is likely that a manufacturer will employ a variety.

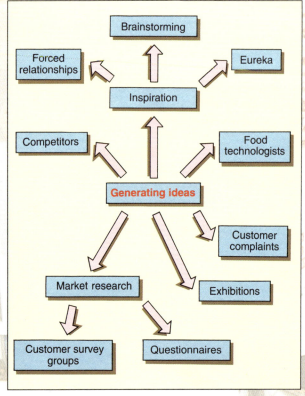

Flashes of
inspiration

Over the years a number of 'creative' approaches have been developed to generate better ideas. These include forced relationships, brainstorming and the 'Eureka' method. They are used to help with thinking around problems and considering them in a different perspective.

Forced relationships

This technique relies upon listing several products and then considering them in relation to each other. In this way a 'new' product can be developed by selling two products together. For instance, it could be possible to suggest some food products from a range that could be paired in order to form part of or a whole meal. Or, one product might be separated into 'two' to make it look new, such as providing the fruit and yogurt in separate compartments rather than mixed.

Tricks of the trade

Consider the food products you may have bought or eaten recently. Have there been occasions when two were bought for the price of one or there were paired items such as stores often use for selling cosmetics and skin/hair care products? Do you think that this method of sales encourages customers to buy items they may not have chosen were they sold singly? Discuss this in a small group. Make a list of items you feel could be sold successfully in this manner.

Brainstorming

Brainstorming is an activity designed to produce as large a number of ideas as possible. Generally a group of six to ten people with no expertise in the product area take part so there is no obvious or agreed answer to the problem. A time limit, such as one hour, is given to each session and ideas are recorded on a flip-chart or tape.

Often with brainstorming one idea will spark off many more. The ideas should be recorded without stopping to question people, so that they flow well. The greater the number of ideas produced the more likelihood there is of useful ideas coming through.

For example, if we were brainstorming ideas around a healthy dessert the following ideas or factors might be suggested: long life, low fat, low cost, individual portions, contain yogurt, natural goodness/flavours, no added sugar, suitable for children, no artificial additives, fruity flavours.

Eureka solutions

These may occur at any time and may be the result of discussion within any department involved in the product development process. One of the most recent innovations has been to consider 'edible packaging'!

·DATA FILE·
Brainstorming

Market research

First you must decide how to research your market, that is the group of possible customers. The research involves finding out the views of possible customers and can be done by **desk research** (see p. 24) or **customer survey**. It is important to find out if there will be a market for your product and gain some idea of the demand; if you produce more than you can sell you may not be able to pay your suppliers, but if you do not produce enough goods your customers will go elsewhere.

Customer surveys

Sometimes a company will ask a store to approach customers about becoming members of a **customer survey group**. They often choose people of the same customer category, such as mothers of young children. The company will contact these customers directly, sometimes several times over a long period, to assess reactions to new products or identify problems or dissatisfaction with an existing product.

Large surveys of customer opinion are usually carried out using **questionnaires**. These are carefully worded sets of questions designed to identify customer preferences and target audiences. A questionnaire can be used to determine whether there is a need for something new, or to decide how an existing product might be improved.

Questionnaires

Design your own questionnaire

Study these two examples of questionnaires. Working in a small group of three or four, try them out and discuss your answers with the rest of your group.

For example, with questionnaire A:
- What do you think influenced your answer?
- Was it because you were asking if you, yourself, would buy them?
- What if you considered the preferences of a different age group?
- What information did it give you?
- How useful was it?

In questionnaire B the type of questions used were different.
- Was this style of questionnaire a bit more useful?
- What information could you get from it ?

A

Consider the following list of items. Decide whether you think they will sell or not and record your opinions. Tick the appropriate box and if you wish make up your own list.

YES NO

- Valentine Cards
- Platform Shoes
- Low-fat Yogurt
- Ready-made party dishes
- Pop/classical mix tapes
- Walkman
- Music Centres
- Soya-based 'meat' products
- Low-alcohol wine

B

Hello, I wonder if you would mind helping me? I am a member of I. Floggitt food store and we are planning to sell a new product in the area but before we do so we want to check on people's reactions.
(picture or description of product)
Male/Female   Occupation
Age group: under 16, 16–25, 26–35, 35 plus.
1. How often would you buy it?
   (If not bought, ask why not?)
2. Where would you buy it?
3. Why would you pay for it?
4. What would you pay for it?
5. Why do you think it could be improved at this stage?
6. Do you think it could be improved at this stage?
7. How does it compare with others?
8. Any other useful suggestions or comments?

Thank you for your time and help.

These two are samples of poor questionnaires. The first includes too many items to ask about and, except for a 'yes' or 'no', gives no indication of the target group that were questioned or why they answered as they did.

Questionnaire B gives a little more information but only about the target group. The layout of questions could be better, so could the style of the questions. When you have worked through this section look at B again and see what you could do to improve it.

A good questionnaire needs to be designed around the product. It will gather useful data which can be analysed to give clear information about the target group and about reactions to the product. It requires short answers, and needs to be fairly simple to do so that it can be given to a large group of people.

What it should find out is whether people **need** the product, whether they **want** it, what they **like** about it, what they would be prepared to **pay** for it, what **benefits** they would expect from it, **how often** they might buy it and **who else** they think might try it.

Just give me the facts!

Some questions are easy to give a 'yes' or 'no' answer to.

This is an example of a **closed** question because there is no opportunity for extending the answer.

> Do you ever eat crisps/snacks?   Yes   No

If the question was put in this way it opens up the possibility to question the 'sometimes' people. You could target this group with a question to find out why they didn't eat these foods more often.

> Do you eat crisps/snacks?   Yes   No   Sometimes

Other questions may carry options.

> Do you like crisps/snacks? All kinds   Some   None

Avoid questions like this. This is an example of an **open** question and could give varied answers which could be difficult to analyse.

> What kinds of crisps/snacks do you like?

However there may be times when you need to ask open questions. It would be better to ask the question like this.

> Which kinds of crisps/snacks do you like? Tick which ones.
>
> crinkle cut crisps [ ]   savoury hoops [ ]
>
> low fat crisps [ ]   cheesy puffs [ ]
>
> waffle crisps [ ]   bombay mix [ ]
>
> ordinary crisps [ ]   peanuts [ ]

This type of question could be extended to find out favourites if worded in this way.

These are called **graded responses**. Does this give you the right type and amount of information?

> Which kinds of crisps/snacks do you like?

	V.much	A little	Not much	Dislike
crinkle cut crisps	[ ]	[ ]	[ ]	[ ]
low fat crisps	[ ]	[ ]	[ ]	[ ]
waffle crisps	[ ]	[ ]	[ ]	[ ]
ordinary crisps	[ ]	[ ]	[ ]	[ ]
savoury hoops	[ ]	[ ]	[ ]	[ ]
cheesy puffs	[ ]	[ ]	[ ]	[ ]
bombay mix	[ ]	[ ]	[ ]	[ ]
peanuts	[ ]	[ ]	[ ]	[ ]

Questionnaires

If a small number of people dislike a snack, is it reasonable to do something about it, such as take that product off the market or develop a new product to meet the need?

What not to ask

- **Leading questions** are usually worded in such a way that the answer you want is in there. The person being questioned will feel compelled to answer 'yes'.

Do you think it is a bad idea to display sweets next to supermarket checkouts?

- **Double questions** make it impossible to decide what the person being questioned has said 'yes' or 'no' to.

  The person may only agree to one of the options, but the question does not allow for this.

Do you think ice creams as well as other snacks should be sold in cinemas during the interval?

- **Ambiguous questions** can result in a wide variety of answers being given, none of which may be the type expected!

What should be done to improve the daytime diet of children?

- **Sensitive questions** sometimes make it impossible for the person to answer honestly.

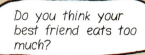

Do you think your best friend eats too much?

How to set out your questionnaire

If your questionnaire requires people to tick boxes then, if all the boxes lie on the right-hand side of the sheet, it is easier to collate the results. The example shown here could be done on a computer.

You may want to enter the results on a **database** in order to analyse your answers. If you are dealing with a large number of questionnaires, the database could be set up in such a way as to identify **fields**, such as gender, age, occupation or shopping habits.

EXAMPLE QUESTIONNAIRE		
Do you ever eat crisps/snacks?	Yes	☐
	No	☐
Do you like crisps/snacks?	All kinds	☐
	Some	☐
	None	☐
Which kinds of crisps/snacks do you like?	Tick 1 or more	
	Crinkle cut crisps	☐
	Low fat crisps	☐
	Waffle crisps	☐
	Ordinary crisps	☐
	Savoury hoops	☐
	Cheesy puffs	☐
	Bombay mix	☐
	Peanuts	☐
	Other	☐

Personal details

These are only needed if necessary to your survey. For example, age is a tricky one. Some people are sensitive about their age, so if it is not necessary then leave it out. If it is important then use categories like this:

11–18   19–25   26–45   45+

With some people it is possible to guess which category they fall into so you do not need to ask.

Generally addresses and names are unimportant so you usually do not ask for these. People are often happier to answer questions if they know they will remain anonymous.

Questionnaires

Test sample

Before you use your questionnaire to gather information you need to check that it asks the right questions. It is best to try it out first on a small group, known as a **test sample**. This is called a **pilot** or a **test run**.

Ask several people who belong to the group you plan to question eventually (such as teenagers, shoppers, etc.) to fill in the questionnaire. Study their answers and also ask their opinion about the questionnaire format.

● Were the questions clear and unbiased?
● Did they allow for opinions to be expressed?
● Were any questions too sensitive?
● Were there any other questions which could be asked?

Remember the difference between open and closed questions. In your test run were your questions of the right type?

Now is the time to alter your questionnaire should it need it. You may need to introduce more open or graded questions to give you more information.

.Hello, I wonder if you would mind helping me? I am a member of I. Floggitt food store and we are planning to sell a new product in the area but before we do so we want to check on people's reactions.
(picture or description of product)
Male/Female Occupation
Age group: under 16, 16–25, 26–35, 35 plus.
1. How often would you buy it?
   (If not bought, ask why not?)
2. Where would you buy it?
3. Why would you pay for it?
4. What would you pay for it?
5. Why do you think it could be improved at this stage?
6. Do you think it could be improved at this stage?
7. How does it compare with others?
8. Any other useful suggestions or comments?

Thank you for your time and help.

More personal questions to the end.

What answers are expected?

Too many open questions Try tick boxes

Change order of questions to put simple and more general first then the specific ones later.

This could be a graded response type question

Try putting possible questions on cards and sorting them into good/bad and not sure piles.

·DATA FILE·

Research techniques
Information systems: databases
Information systems: spreadsheets
Information systems: wordprocessing

Questionnaires

Did it work?

Once you are satisfied with the layout and format of your questionnaire you need to choose a large enough group to give you sufficient data to analyse. This is known as the **sample**.

How large should the sample be?

- Too small will not give enough data to analyse.
- Too large will take too long to question and analyse.

The time in which you have to complete your survey and analysis may help you to decide the size of your sample.
   Next you need to decide whether your sample will be random or structured.

- In a **random** sample you may question every fourth person in your class or in a particular street, regardless of occupation, age or gender. For example if carrying out some research in school, a random sample of 10% would look like this.
- In a **structured** sample you would question people of a specific representative group, such as teenagers, vegetarians, pensioners or car drivers.

School	Number	Sample
Total	1400	140
Boys	700	70
Girls	700	70
Each year group	100	10

Final checklist

General points before you start.

- Where are you going to conduct your survey?
- Who are you going to be questioning?
- Have you got permission (if necessary)?
- Do not knock on doors or go into stranger's houses.
- Do not argue or disagree with people you are questioning.
- Do not answer back if someone is rude to you, go on to the next person.

BE POLITE! People will be happier to take part!!

What did you find out?

The raw data from the completed questionnaires must be collated and analysed before you can draw any conclusions . The answers could be grouped and displayed as tables, graphs, and charts. (See the *Datafile* sheets 5–8 and 56–63.) These will make it easier to answer questions like 'Which type is most popular?', and maybe even 'Why is one kind not popular?'. These answers will help you to judge where there is a gap in the market and what is most likely to succeed in filling that gap.

Age	Most favourite snack
3-6 yrs	savoury hoops
7-10 yrs	cheesy puffs
11-14 yrs	low fat crisps
Mums and Dads	peanuts
Grans and Grandads	ordinary crisps
Other	waffle crisps.

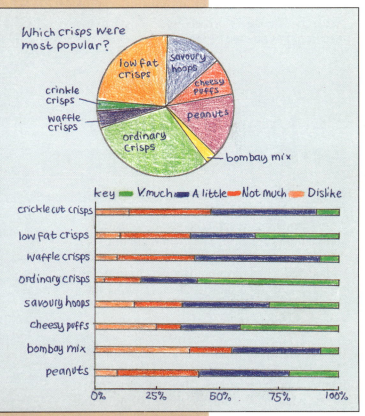

Which crisps were most popular?

key — Vmuch — A little — Not much — Dislike

Asking the right questions

In small groups prepare your own market research questionnaire.

Choose a well-known product, like coffee, snack bars or cereals, and find out who likes it and why. Think of at least five questions, including open and closed ones. Remember the simpler the questions, the more you can ask and the easier it will be to carry out and analyse. Try it out on at least two people outside school to test whether you have phrased the questions well. Then choose your sample (will it be structured or random?), carry out the survey and analyse the results.

Did the questionnaire provide the sort of information which would be useful to a manufacturer?

Desk research

Desk research will examine and collate the market research sources such as customer group surveys and questionnaires. Valuable information is also provided by independent market research companies, and this will need to be analysed also. This is quite a cheap way of doing market research. The hard work of 'field research' has already been done.

Customer complaints and suggestions

Following up on customer complaints,' whether from the Customer Relations Department or in-store complaints procedure, can be a useful source of information. They will highlight problems with existing products which can be considered when developing a new or improved product. It is important to check carefully the frequency and validity of complaints and not react to just one or two!

Let's assume that this is the fifth letter the Complaints Department have had this week highlighting these points. They will have to decide what, as a company, should be done and who would be responsible for carrying it through. Also, they will need to draft a reply to the customer as good public relations (PR) is important. This could be supported with some goodies or a special offer as a gesture of thanks for the customer's concern.

Sunny Cottage
Pie Lane
Staffs
SDT EP3
1.4.92

Customer Complaints
Good Health Products Ltd.
Farm Lane Way
Kings Town
KS12 KS3

Dear Sir or Madam,

As I am a regular purchaser of many of your products I feel I must write to complain about your most recent product Oriental Savoury Rice.

On the two occasions I have bought it from your store, I have found the following:

1. The separated containers in the carton do not prevent the juice from the meat section going into the rice. It is therefore messy in appearance and soggy before being re-heated.

2. The packaging specifies it contains two servings. Though my husband and I do not have large appetites we find that there is barely enough for us to have a good taster.

3. You claim that it is made with exotic herbs and spices and resembles a dish of eastern origin. To our taste it is very bland and insipid and would question the authenticity of this recipe.

I am disappointed that I must write in this way but usually I find your products very pleasing, tasty and good value for money. I look forward to hearing from you very soon.

Your faithfully
A.J. Moan (Mrs)

The right reply

Assume you are the member of the Complaints Department who was given the letter from Mrs Moan. Draft a suitable reply, bearing in mind you must keep the good name of the company. Also, draft a report to the development team suggesting improvements that could be made to the product.

Food technologists

Food technologists are employed by a company to devise new products as well as to suggest improvements with existing products. They are expected to be able to give advice on how to improve the quality of the food, how to reduce the cost of making it and be aware of new ideas that come along in the industry. One such idea was the invention of the 'healthy' alternative to sugar, aspartame (brand name NutraSweet), which is found in many food products today.

Novel ideas for food

You are a member of a group of food technologists who have been directed to think of new ideas for mini fruit cakes for special occasions. This could include new ways of preparing the cakes, different kinds of decoration or packaging.

In a small group try to come up with some exciting and attractive ideas to present to the company's development team. Try your ideas out on the rest of the class.

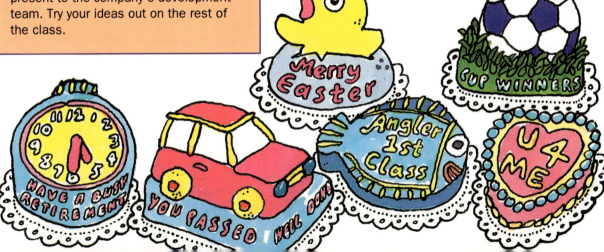

Know your competitors

It is important for a manufacturer to keep a watchful eye on competitors and what they are developing. Questions that would be asked are:

- Who will we be competing with?
- What do they make?
- What prices do they charge?
- What are they good at?
- What are they not so good at ?
- Why will our product be better than theirs?
- Why do people buy from them?
- Do they offer any extras?
- What can we learn from them?

Answers to these may help to give ideas of where there is a gap in the market and how to beat the competition in filling that gap. Also, sales of new products launched by competitors will usually be monitored to assess why they are bought, by whom and when.

By evaluating a competitor's successful product it may be possible to make limited changes and generate a similar product for your own company. It is also likely that big companies may use the same manufacturer for many of their products.

Companies prize the secrecy that surrounds their development work, but it is said that visits to suppliers can be useful to look for opportunities. It is surprising what information is left lying about because of familiarity!

Looking at chilled foods

Visit two of your local stores/food suppliers. List the range of chilled foods on offer in each. How similar are they? They may be made by the same manufacturer.

Set out your findings ▶ like this.

Company	Type of food	Cost	Main ingredient	Type of appeal	Comments

Exhibitions

Exhibitions provide the opportunity to look at ideas for packaging, labelling, display of products as well as the products themselves. Contacts with new prospective suppliers can begin here and, with the wider market now available through the EC membership, it may be possible to make such contacts throughout Europe.

Concept screening

When the development team have collected together all the ideas (concepts) from all the different sources, they must sift throught them to separate the good ones from the bad. This is known as **concept screening**. They must decide whether the product will sell well (be economically viable), whether it will be possible to find suppliers for new raw materials and whether the company will be able to make the product.

Bright ideas

Your research has come up with the following ideas as areas for development. In a small group, discuss whether you think any of these might be successful. You might like to take one of these further and think of a range of suitable products to develop.
- Edible jewellery
- Re-usable packaging
- Packaging that dissolves
- A sweetener that does not affect the teeth and is itself a natural food

From the results the development team will determine a concept for a 'new' product and evaluate it to see if it fulfils the original criteria required, such as:
- suitable for a snack,
- healthy food bar,
- good 'green' image,
- can be sold singly.

It has been estimated that for every 60 ideas generated:
- only 12 get through screening to check their compatibility with the company objectives and resources,
- of these 12, only 7 may remain once it is seen how much profit they will generate,
- only 3 may survive the product development stage,
- only 2 will survive test marketing,
- 1 may prove to be commercially successful.

Developing a food
PRODUCT

There are two major phases in developing the food product:
- **developing the food itself,**
- **developing the packaging, advertising and labelling that is needed to sell the food.**

The detailed work in developing the food is done by the food technologists. They investigate how to make the food, known as **prototyping**, determine the quantities of ingredients, list the ingredients and nutritional information for the labelling, and work out the **shelf-life**, that is how long the product will remain in good condition before it is sold. Then suppliers need to be found for the ingredients. Some of this requires laboratory checks to be made on the food. The factories which will make the food will have to be thoroughly inspected for health and safety aspects.

This whole process may take up to three months and will involve teams from different departments investigating their own aspects of the process. Yet everything must come together at the right time to prevent costly delays and ensure success.

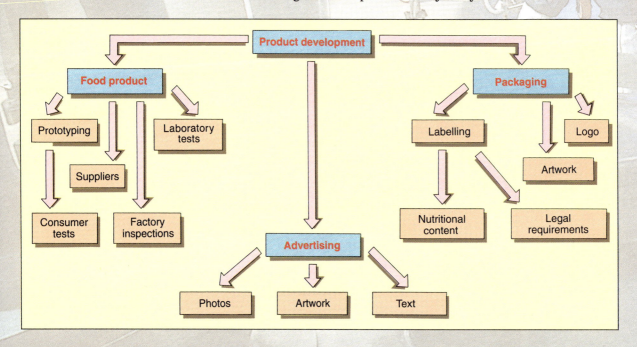

It is in these early stages that companies use diagrams such as **Gantt charts** or **critical path network diagrams**. Gantt charts are diagrams which show not only what has to be done, but in what order and how long the different stages will take. They also allow you to plan which activities can be done at the same time.

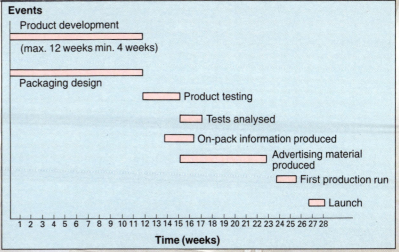

A critical path analysis diagram is even more detailed, showing individual tasks, the **earliest date** on which they can start and the **latest date** on which they can be completed. It may give a **critical path**, that is the tasks which must be done in sequence at the right time so as not to hold up the rest of the process.

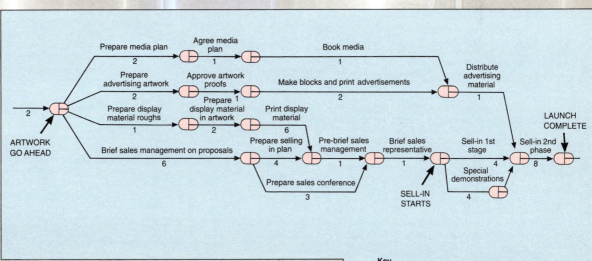

Here is part of a critical path diagram used by Sainsbury in their production process. This part refers to advertising and is only a small part of the complete process.

ESD (earliest start date) is the earliest time when an activity can start so that all necessary previous activities will have been completed.
LT is the latest time by which an activity must be reached if the process is to be kept on schedule.

Producing your own food product

The process you can go through in school can be very similar to the commercial process just described, though you will not need to do some stages, such as factory inspection. Let's assume that some market research has shown that there is a market gap where any of the three following items could be developed:

- a convenience vegetarian meal,
- a healthy snack for a teenager,
- a range of savoury yogurts for dips.

Working in small groups, choose one of these to develop.

Here are some areas you may need to consider.

- Who is your target audience?
- What materials will you need – are they readily available?
  – are they easily stored?
- Are there any hidden or extra costs?
- Would a spreadsheet help to record costs and price the product?
- Can you carry out a test run with a sample from your target group? (Remember to evaluate your work against your specification.)
- Can you identify a suitable portion size – how many is it meant to serve?
- Can you produce alternatives for consumer testing? (This might be different possible foods within the specification or different size portions.)
- Are you aiming to design a range of related products, or will this be a 'one–off'?

·DATA FILE·

Information systems:
spreadsheets
Nutritional guidelines
Food additives
Special diets

Where do I begin?

You could start with a food base such as rice, pasta, yogurt or bread from which to design your product. Or you could start with an existing recipe, make it, evaluate it and make changes to it where necessary.

You might start with a particular type of product or target group, or this could come later when ideas begin to develop.

Think about the criteria that your product should be judged against: cost, nutritional value, sensory appeal, appearance, novelty value, etc. At some point you will need to produce a **specification** for the product so that it can be evaluated.

You may decide to divide your team up so that pairs can look at different aspects of the process. The team can then make a final presentation at the end of the time available. This will require careful time planning. You could use a planning chart, such as a sequence diagram, flow chart or Gantt chart, to help you to organise your time

Products designed from a rice base

Consumer testing

Once you have made your food(s) you should try them out on a test sample. If your target group is not members of your age group, ask your teacher whether you will be able to try your products out on your target group.

 Safety and hygiene are very important. If the food is not to be tested straight away, make sure it is stored properly and not for too long. Any spoons or lollipop sticks used for testing should be used by one person only and then thrown away.

As you have a specification for your product, you should be able to set criteria to see if it has been a success. It is not enough just to ask people if they like it and how much they would pay for it. Make up a questionnaire to ask specific questions to judge reactions to the product and analyse the results to see whether your product would satisfy the market gap.

   Your teacher will be able to help you work out a suitable type of test to do the analysis.

Packaging the product

During the time that the food product is being developed the technologists and designers will investigate suitable packaging. For this to be done it must be known what form the final product will take, its size and consistency and whether it will be sold as a single item or in multiples.

Technologists and designers must also think about the materials for the packet design, logos and advertising. They must decide about any nutritional, legal or recipe information that is to be on the packaging and also any artwork or photography that is going to be used.

Did you know that?

● in 1986, in the UK alone, £5.3 billion was spent by manufacturers on packaging!
● 60% of all packaging is for food!

The way in which food has been presented to the consumer has changed a great deal over the last few years, and is big business for those companies involved. At one time the food on sale would be displayed unwrapped in shops and only weighed and sold when wrapped up for the consumer to take home. Now most food we buy is protected by packaging.

The main purpose behind packaging food is to:
● keep the food from spoiling,
● protect the food from structural damage,
● guarantee safety and hygiene,
● help stop people from tampering with the food,
● allow efficient transportation from place of manufacture to the point of sale,
● identify and describe the contents for the consumer,
● help marketing and increase sales.

What's in the box?

Draw up a list of everyday items that you can buy that are packed. What was the specific need for that packaging? What problems do you think the manufacturer had to overcome?

As well as outside packaging there may be a need to protect the contents inside. In packaging that can be used in a microwave or conventional oven the food is usually placed in a formed plastic dish and covered with a protective film.

Have you ever come across a case of 'overpackaging', where there has been little necessity for the amount used?

Organise a collection of samples of different types of packaging. Include things other than food items. Look at each sample individually. Do you think it performed its function well?

Does the type of packaging used pose a problem for our environment, or could it be recycled? See if you can find out about the type of materials used for the packaging, have their use in any way damaged our environment?

When designing packaging for your product you should ask yourself whether your ideas are environmentally friendly. Card is made from trees and plastics from oil, both of which are valuable natural resources. Some European countries now try to 'design out' the packaging so that the amount that has to be recycled is kept to a minimum.

Tesco is a company who looks carefully at the materials they use for packaging. Without altering their product performance they state that:

- 'a change in thickness of plastic film around their kitchen towels and toilet tissue will result in a saving of over 60 tonnes of polyethylene in a year.
- using recycled board in their tissue and washing powder boxes will save over 300 tonnes of new board in one year.'

Their information leaflets are also published and printed on recycled paper.

Looking at the packaging you have collected can you find evidence of other manufacturers taking the same steps?

Throw it or save it?

If packaging materials cannot be re-used it means they need to be disposed of.

Many local authorities are only too conscious of the problem of disposing of our 'throw away' packaging materials. Some materials can be recycled and authorities often set up collection points in convenient locations for the consumer, such as the car parks of major supermarkets, or on specified days in a village hall car park. We are being encouraged to think more about the items we so readily throw away and to consider how we dispose of them.

Check in your local area to see if there are recycling facilities. What materials are your authority sending for recycling? See if you can find out where they go and what happens to them.

In European countries where they 'design out' packaging, they also suggest good ideas for other uses for the packaging so that it is used to best effect. Supermarkets even have recycling collection points so that people can remove packaging before they take the product home. You may be able to develop your designs with these ideas in mind.

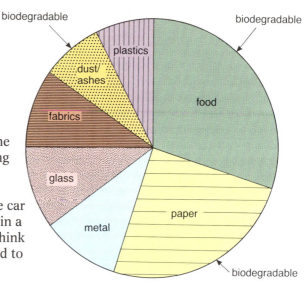

biodegradable
plastics
dust/ashes
fabrics
biodegradable
food
glass
paper
metal
biodegradable

Do you recycle?

Your local authority has approached your group for help. They have found that public response to their recycling campaign is poor. They ask you to devise an advertising strategy which could be used countywide using the local media as economically as possible. Working in small groups, plan such a scheme and prepare a presentation to be given to representatives of the authority. This must show samples of the publicity materials you would suggest and an estimated cost for the campaign.

· D A T A   F I L E ·
Biosystems: household waste

Designing your packaging

Collect sample boxes that you can find at home. Carefully undo the seams where the box sides have been stuck together and look at the shape of the box net. Note where the gluing tabs have been placed.

If you look at a selection of different food packages you will normally find that there is a picture of the food product on the front and the background design may well set the scene of the food's origin or content. It is also necessary to have an idea of the name of the product as this may influence your surface design.

On the face of it

You are now going to design the packaging for the food product you developed earlier. Your teacher should be able to give you copies of nets for two boxes. Using an old biro pen score along all the dotted lines. Cut out on the solid lines and fold into shape. Do not stick them together until all surface detail has been added.

Think about the type of food that will go in the box. It may suggest ideas for a suitable surface design. Don't forget to leave space for the necessary labels. Information on these is given in the 'Labelling' section later. Think about who will buy the food and who it must appeal to.

To create original surface designs refer to the section on 'Frinton Ferries' in the *Key stage 3 core*. It will give you some ideas of how to produce drawings for original designs from first-hand observations.

What's in a name?

Your next stage is to choose a suitable name for your product. You could do this by giving a group of fellow pupils a description of your product, its content and its varied uses. Using the brainstorm technique ask them to suggest suitable ideas for names. Having drawn up a list you could then, as a design team, choose the most suitable for your product.

Methods of transferring designs to boxes

The design and any labelling to go on the carton is best added when the net shape is marked out, but preferably before it is cut out. How are you going to do any pattern or illustration? Think about this carefully before you begin.

If you are only making one package the simplest way of carrying out your surface decoration would be to illustrate graphically your design onto coloured paper then carefully stick this onto the net.

If making more than one package you could make a decorative border or surface pattern by using block or lino prints.

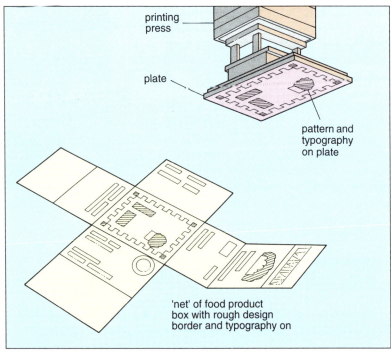

printing press

plate

pattern and typography on plate

'net' of food product box with rough design border and typography on

For large-scale package production it is best to use block, screen or pad printing. This also allows you to introduce a variety of colours to your decoration. The *Datafile* sheets 39–41 can give you guidance on doing this.

As well as the decorative effects you want on your package you need to decide how you are going to transfer letters or wording. Consider suitable typefaces and the use of colour or shade. It is best to spend time investigating this and making some samples for your team to decide from.

·D A T A   F I L E·
Printing techniques
Lettering

Vacuum-forming inner cartons

Manufacturers use injection moulded or vacuum-formed containers. Many schools have vacuum-forming equipment but few will be able to make injection mould containers.

You could design a container to hold your food product. First, you will need to make a **former** for making the vacuum-formed tray. Before deciding on the shape of your formed dish, look at the variety used. Some are made up of separate compartments holding different parts of the meal. Decide on the amount of food it needs to hold and protect.

Medium density fibre board (MDF) is ideal for making the formers but it is also possible to use clay, plaster of paris or builders' plaster successfully. Thermoplastic must be used for the vacuum-formed tray.

You will need instruction and guidance regarding the **safe** and **efficient** use of the equipment **before** you begin.

Make sure that:
- the shape of the former makes it easy for the shaped plastic to be removed, this includes the **slope**, or **draft angle**, of the sides,
- the temperature of the plastic is right – it is crucial for making a good shape,
- there are air holes drilled at the base of the former where a hollow curve will form,
- surface patterns are well defined so that they come out on the finished shape.

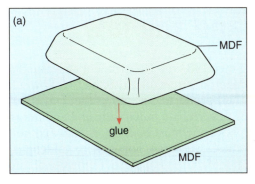

(a)

MDF

glue

MDF

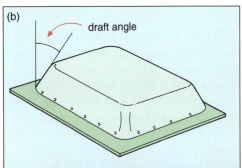

(b) draft angle

⚠️ Special food grade plastic should be used (polypropylene) for vacuum-forming. This can then be used in microwave ovens.

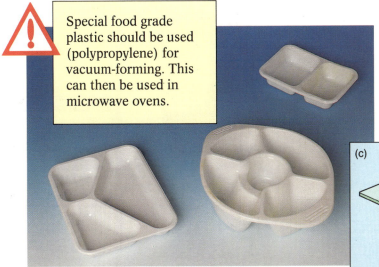

(c)

waste

carton

Labelling and the law

Since 1984 the Government has issued guidelines which manufacturers are expected to follow when labelling their products. The aim is that you should know what it is that you are purchasing and any information given on packaging must be clear, factual and not misleading. The Government hopes these guidelines will encourage manufacturers to present nutritional information in a standard way so that you can compare foods more easily.

The main points you will see on a label are:
- the name and description of the food,
- what it is made from,
- how long it can be kept and under what conditions,
- its weight, volume or number in the pack,
- its place(s) of origin,
- preparation and cooking instructions where necessary,
- the name and address of the manufacturer, packer or seller, in case the consumer wants any further information or needs to complain about the product.

In addition there has been an increase in the number of items that display:

- nutritional information,
- claim particular benefits for a food,

and most recently:
- environmental benefits.

By studying packaging from different types of food products we can learn a good deal about them. We can also learn to recognise the type of information we are usually given. Look at these samples. They clearly show the statutory information the law requires.

FOOD SENSE

BEST BEFORE & USE BY

A GUIDE TO THE CHANGES

MAFF

PAXO SAGE & ONION Stuffing Mix

COOKING INSTRUCTIONS

PREPARATION
For 4 servings, place the contents of the sachet into a large bowl, add 250ml (½ pint) boiling water, stir well and allow to stand for 5 minutes. Allow a little longer if stuffing a joint of meat or the neck end cavity of poultry.

TO BAKE
Cook in a greased ovenproof dish for 20-30 minutes at 220°C, 425°F, Gas Mark 7.

TO MICROWAVE
(650W) cook in a heatproof microwaveable dish, on HIGH for 3½ minutes. Crisp under a hot grill for a few minutes before serving.

TO GRILL
Make up with 200ml (8fl oz) boiling water, cool and shape into individual portions. Brush with butter and grill each side for 3 minutes.

PAXO TIP
For a richer, crisper stuffing add a knob of butter with the boiling water.

6 Chocolate Chip Tracker

Chewy Oat, Nuts and Crisped Rice Bar with Chocolate Chips

NUTRITION INFORMATION	PER 27g	PER 100g
Energy kcal	132	490
kJ	553	2049
Protein	2.5g	9.1g
Carbohydrate	15.2g	56.3g
Fat	7.3g	26.9g
VITAMINS		
Niacin	0.49mg	1.80mg
Thiamin	0.04mg	0.15mg
MINERALS		
Calcium	13.01mg	48.2mg
Iron	0.38mg	1.4mg

INGREDIENTS

Muesli, (Rolled Oats, Peanuts, Crisped Rice, Hazelnuts), Glucose Syrup, Hydrogenated Vegetable Oil, Chocolate Chips, Sweetened Condensed Skimmed Milk, Butter Oil, Glycerol, Icing Sugar, Brown Sugar, Fat Reduced Cocoa, Salt, Emulsifier: Lecithin

Chocolate Chips Contain Emulsifier: Lecithin

INGREDIENTS:
Skimmed Milk, Sugar, Butter Fat, Vegetable Fat, Condensed Skimmed Milk, Glucose Syrup, Cocoa Powder, Emulsifiers: Mono and Di-glycerides of fatty Acids, Lecithin; Stabilisers: Sodium Alginate, Carrageenan, Locust Bean Gum, Guar Gum; Flavourings.

CONTAINS NO ARTIFICIAL COLOURS OR PRESERVATIVES

NUTRITION INFORMATION
(TYPICAL VALUES)

EACH 100ml OF THIS PRODUCT GIVES YOU:		PER EIGHTH OF GATEAU
ENERGY	538 kJ	506 kJ
	129 kcal	121 kcal
PROTEIN	1.7 g	1.6 g
CARBOHYDRATE	11.0 g	10.3 g
(of which sugars)	11.0 g	10.3 g
FAT	8.7 g	8.2 g
(of which saturates)	8.7 g	8.2 g
SODIUM	Trace	Trace
DIETARY FIBRE	Trace	Trace

121 CALORIES PER EIGHTH OF GATEAU

Produced in Germany for Iceland Frozen Foods plc, Deeside, Clwyd CH5 2NW

FIBREBOARD PACKAGING

103

Names

The labels must clearly show what food it is. If the name states 'strawberry milk shake' then it must contain strawberries. If it says 'strawberry flavour' then the flavouring is more likely to be artificially produced from chemicals. Likewise food that has been treated to add flavour or prolong keeping quality should be labelled 'processed', such as smoked bacon, canned or dried fruit. The label must state if the food belongs to a particular group or variety, such as Granny Smith apples, Cos lettuce or King Alfred potatoes. Pasta may be spaghetti or cannelloni; rice could be patna or pudding.

If the product has a brand name, this must be clearly described on the package. Look at these brand names. Do they give you some idea of the product?

Ingredients

Manufacturers must list ingredients in foods in descending order of weight of the individual ingredients, but do not have to state individual weight. If part of a dish contains a processed food such as pasta, which itself contains several ingredients, these must also be included.
Any items which could not be classified as foods must also be listed, such as additives used to preserve or enhance the dish.

Keeping conditions

Most food items now carry a date mark. This indicates the freshness of a product and allows us to use it when it is at its best. It also enables the retailer to keep stocks up to date.

- **Best before**
  If it is possible to keep the food for longer than three months only the month and year will be given. If the food needs to be used within a three-month period then the date and month will be given.
- **Sell by date**
  Used generally on perishable foods. Not only will it state the date by which the product must be sold, but will also tell you within how many days after purchase the food must be eaten.
- **Use by date**
  These often replace sell by dates on highly perishable foods

·DATA FILE·
Nutritional guidelines
Special diets
Food: storage

Weight, volume or number

It is required that for most foods labels should state the quantity either by **net weight**, that is the weight of the food product without the packaging, such as 283 g (10 oz), or by volume such as 568 ml (1 pint). The '℮' that often accompanies this shows that the EC system of quality control applies to this product.

Sometimes it is more useful to know the number you are buying. For instance, when buying a 'jumbo' pack of potato crisps the outer packaging will state the number of smaller packs it contains and will also give the required contents information. With ready chilled food items it is possible that the package will say how many persons the pack will serve.

How to cook

For ready prepared foods the instructions for preparation and cooking are all important. There have been many cases in recent years where consumers have not followed instructions to the letter and these have resulted in cases of food poisoning. The instructions must be clear and concise and take account of different methods of cooking.

COOKING INSTRUCTIONS

MICROWAVE OVEN Microwave ovens vary in performance. The following is a guide only and based on a modern 650W oven. Heating time must be increased for lower powered ovens. Remove sleeve. Pierce the film in several places and cook on full power for 3½ minutes. Allow to stand for 1 minute before serving. Check that the food is piping hot throughout. If not, re-cover and heat for a further brief period.

CONVENTIONAL OVEN (adjust for fan assisted ovens) Remove sleeve. Do not remove or pierce film. Place on a baking tray in a preheated oven at 180°C, 350°F, gas mark 4 for 20-25 minutes.

Nutritional information

This describes the food product in terms of energy content and amounts of basic food groups (protein, carbohydrate and fat). It sometimes includes details such as vitamin content or amounts of saturated and unsaturated fats. The information given must be correct and will state the content for 100 g of that food. This can be very useful for consumers, especially if they are on a restricted or special diet.

HOW TO COOK
For best results cook from frozen

SHALLOW FRY. Heat ¼" cooking oil in a frying pan. Fry cheeseburgers over a medium heat for approximately 8—10 minutes, turning occasionally until brown

GRILL. Preheat grill to medium/high heat. Grill cheeseburgers for approximately 15-18 minutes, turning occasionally until brown.

MICROWAVE (650w) Preheat a browning griddle according to manufacturers instructions. Place 2 cheeseburgers onto the griddle and cook on high, power level 9, for approximately 3½ minutes, turning halfway through the cooking time.
WARNING: THE CHEESE WILL BE VERY HOT ONCE COOKED.

Health foods

SUITABLE FOR VEGETARIANS

Claims for being beneficial to any particular group of people, such as diabetics or slimmers, require the product to meet strict criteria and must not be misleading.

GLUTEN FREE

Some products may claim that organically grown foods have been used, or that the packaging can be or has been recycled. This is to attract customers who care about the environment.

Say it with a label

When considering the nutritional information you are going to put onto your label you will first need to make a list of the ingredients used and their quantity. Once you have made your trial dish you can measure its final weight. You can then determine its nutritional content for each 100 g present. Books such as *Food Tables* by Bender and Bender or *Manual of Nutrition* from HMSO will give you detailed nutritional breakdown of any of the ingredients. Think how difficult it must be for a blind or partially sighted person to read this information. Can you think of a way to overcome this?

Findus
LeanCuisine®
CHICKEN CHASSEUR WITH RICE
For Healthy Appetites
LOW IN FAT & SATURATES
CONTROLLED SODIUM
APPROVED BY THE FAMILY HEART ASSOCIATION AS PART OF A LOW FAT DIET
NEW
Microwaveable

Barcoding

The use of scanning at checkouts means that computers can be used in stores to closely monitor the products sold. Scanning may be by hand-held devices or fixed laser scanner. These read the barcode on the labelling on most consumer goods.

The barcode symbol consists of a series of bars and spaces of varying width. When a scanner reads a barcode it identifies the contrast between the light and dark areas of the lines. Black and white give the best contrast because white reflects most light while black reflects little or no light. The barcode allows the computer to recognise the numbers and therefore identify the product.

Once the number is read, the scanner transmits it to the store's computer which instantly relays the product description and current price to the checkout machine. This results in an itemised till receipt for the customer. For the store, this instant recording makes it easier to monitor what is being sold and which stocks are running low and need reordering.

Large companies, such as Sainsbury, also have the information relayed directly to the central computer at their headquarters. This up-to-the-minute sales information from all the stores is used by the central computer for an entire business information system involving stock control, ordering, special offers, promotions and advertising. With new products it also gives a global view of their sales pattern and in turn their success, which can be used to determine if any changes are needed in response to consumer reactions.

Barcoding can also be used in other situations, such as library bookings (loans), security systems (pass cards) and for payment (credit/telephone cards).

Barcode reader

Commercial barcode readers are very expensive. This is a result of the accuracy needed to detect very small differences in line width and position.

It is quite straightforward to make a barcode reader with inexpensive sensors but the final barcode will be large in size to match the coarse resolution of the sensor. However, the techniques involved are the same as those employed in commercial systems.

Modern readers use scanning lasers which are well beyond the scope of work in schools at this time. Simpler commercial readers of the pen type use a 'swipe' technique which is more practical to consider now.

Using a reflective opto-sensor and some means of moving the sensor over a barcode or vice versa it is possible to use a computer to interpret the signals and come up with a number or product name.

Let's look at a possible system to achieve this.

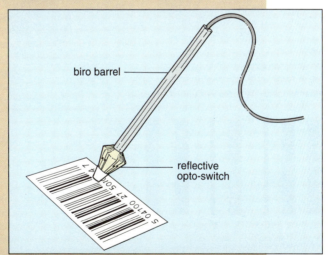

biro barrel

reflective opto-switch

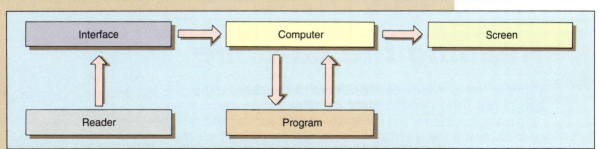

Interface → Computer → Screen

Reader → Program

Each sub-system needs to be designed to operate efficiently so that the total system works effectively. Let's look at each part in turn.

Make your own reader

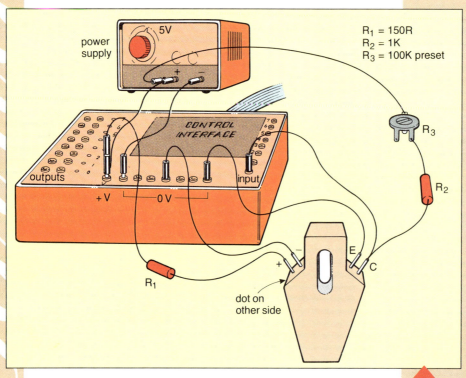

power supply 5V

$R_1 = 150R$
$R_2 = 1K$
$R_3 = 100K$ preset

CONTROL INTERFACE

outputs

input

+ V   0 V

R_3

R_2

E

C

+

R_1

dot on other side

This shows one type of commonly available reflective opto-sensor and how to wire it up to detect barcodes.

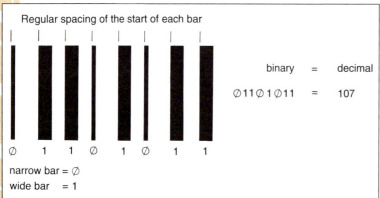

Regular spacing of the start of each bar

binary	=	decimal
$\emptyset$11$\emptyset$1$\emptyset$11	=	107

$\emptyset$ 1   1 $\emptyset$ 1 $\emptyset$ 1   1

narrow bar = $\emptyset$
wide bar   = 1

Reading the barcode

With a simple barcode a binary number can be coded using bars of two distinct widths (**thick** and **thin**).

To make it easier for the computer to read such a code we need to control the speed at which the sensor passes over the bars. Two methods could provide starting points for this aspect of the project. The barcode could be read either by (a) moving the reader over the barcode, or (b) moving the barcode over the reader.

(a) A buggy with a reflective opto-sensor mounted underneath can be made to 'drive' over the barcode and the resulting signal fed into the computer via an interface.

(b) A system such as this can read the code on security tags or labels which are fed through the rollers.

The signals from the slotted opto-switch will need to pass through an interface to make them suitable for the computer to read.

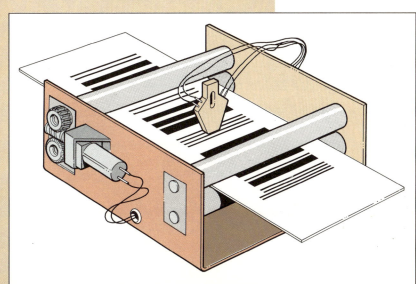

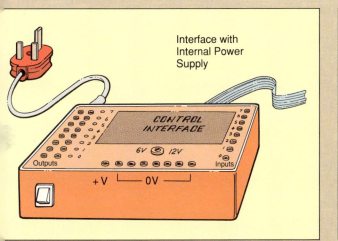

Interface with Internal Power Supply

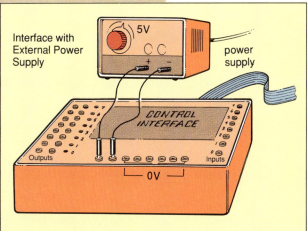

Interface with External Power Supply

Computer program

Because of the difficulty of programming in different languages a flow diagram method will be used to describe a software system which could be used to read barcodes with the hardware already discussed.

Main program

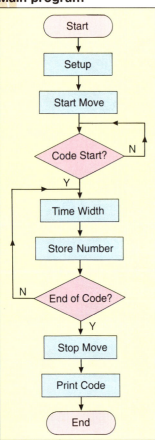

Each part of the program can now be **broken down into smaller parts.**

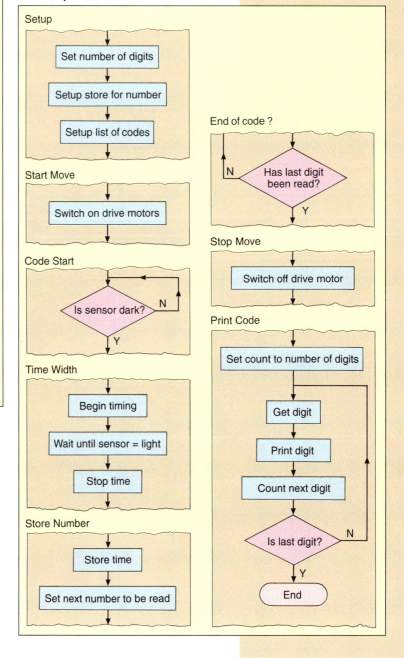

Further ideas

Sensors

A range of sensors could be used but few are as precise as the reflective opto-sensor.

Rotation sensing

Instead of driving the reader at a fixed speed across the barcode, a sensor attached to a freely rotating wheel could detect the width of bars.

Programming

These areas are possible extensions of the initial program:
● convert binary number into decimal number,
● convert number into product name,
● combine several names into product list,
● allocate prices to products.

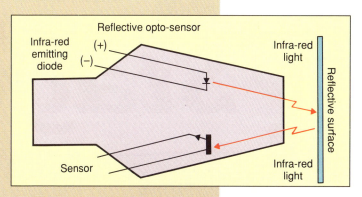

Reflective opto-sensor

Infra-red emitting diode

(+)
(−)

Infra-red light

Reflective surface

Sensor

Infra-red light

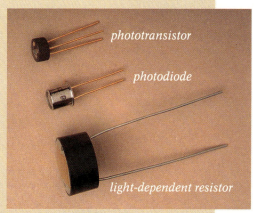

phototransistor

photodiode

light-dependent resistor

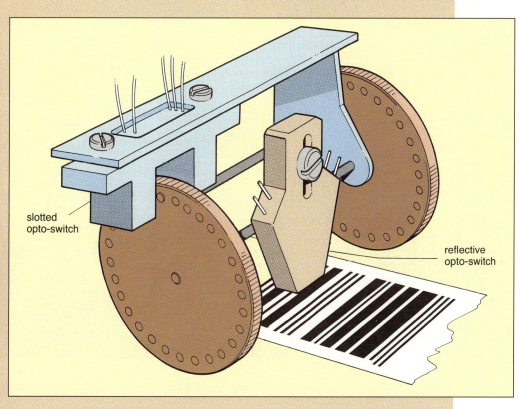

slotted opto-switch

reflective opto-switch

THE FINAL Stages

The new food product has been finalised, suitable packaging designed and the labelling agreed upon. The final stages in the food development process are the first production run, the advertising campaign and the product launch.

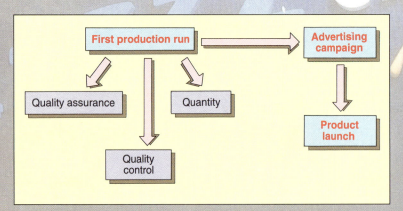

First production run → Advertising campaign

First production run → Quality assurance

First production run → Quantity

First production run → Quality control

Advertising campaign → Product launch

First production run

During this trial a thorough check is carried out of the premises where the food is to be produced. Companies such as Sainsbury or Tesco lay down strict quality criteria for the companies producing food on their behalf. Suppliers are required to confirm that they have carried out an internal quality control audit and have taken any steps found to be necessary to put right anything which does not comply with the rules. Further development does not take place until this has been done.

During the production run **quality assurance** will be carried out, that is tests throughout all stages of production to make sure standards are being met. At the end of the run tests will be made on the product to check, for instance, that individual items are the right weight. This is known as **quality control**.

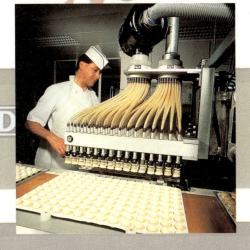

ADVERTISING

Advertising is usually to attract people to buy a product. Millions of pounds are spent each year to convince us that each manufacturers' product is the best one for us to buy. We may feel that our choice is 'free' but we are influenced by adverts and publicity. Adverts should be neither false nor misleading and the Advertising Standards Authority lays down standards which must be followed. Anyone can complain to them if they think an advert is misleading or offensive.

Good advertising campaigns will not only increase sales of a particular product, but also raise people's awareness towards the company which makes it. The aim should be to make the company and product name instantly recognisable and associated with value for money.

Adverts may be put on television, radio, in cinema, newspapers, magazines, posters, hoardings, showcards and point-of-sale leaflets.

Advertising Standards Authority Ltd.
Dept. 2, Brook House,
Torrington Place,
London WC1E 7HN.

You must remember this!

As a group draw up descriptions of advertisements that you have come across in each of the media methods mentioned above. Can you say what in particular makes each advertisement stand out in your memory?

Types of advertising

These are general terms used in the industry to classify the type of advertisement:

- **informative** — helps the consumer make an informed choice,
- **generic** — promotion of a product by a number of advertisers,
- **classified** — small advertisements arranged under different headings,
- **persuasive** — using 'persuasive' images or language,
- **competitive** — one firm trying to expand market share at expense of competitors,
- **point-of-sale** — information cards or leaflets where the products are sold,
- **direct mail** — advertising literature put through letter box,
- **corporate** — building up the image of the company more than selling a product.

New Viennetta Cappuccino.
Guaranteed to cause a stir

The lowest of the low fat spreads.

If it doesn't have the Heinz label on the outside, it won't have Heinz beans on the inside.

St. Ivel Gold has half the fat of sunflower margarines.

Grouping advertisements

Find your own examples for each type of advertisement mentioned above and say what aspect of them appealed to you or caught your attention.

Other reasons to advertise

Advertising (vertical sidebar text)

Although we generally associate advertising with selling products, it has many other and varied uses.

- **Industry** perhaps to attract investors, to advertise vacancies in the firm or to highlight changes in the company.
- **Future events** such as in the theatre and cinema, for exhibitions and charity events.
- **To attract support** such as environmental groups, political parties and anti-vivisection groups.
- **Education** such as courses in colleges, universities and evening classes.
- **Personal** for celebrating an event or to sell property.
- **Charitable** as in requests for support and funds.
- **To attract** more viewers, readers or listeners to different media.
- **Public information** regarding the law, people's rights and local services.

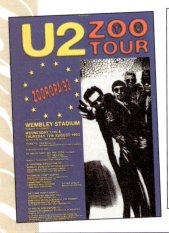

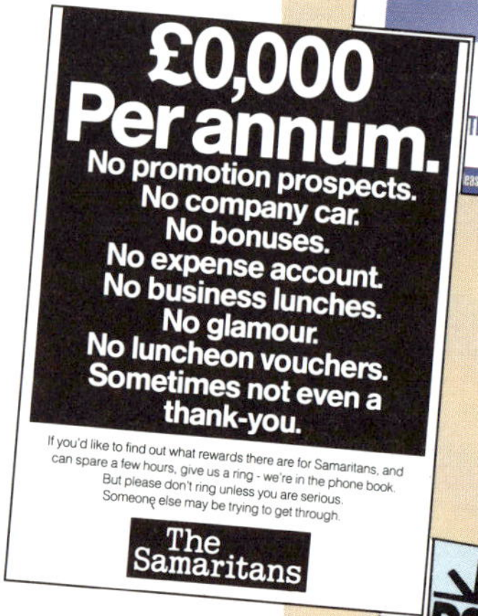

Advertising types and audiences

Working in groups of three or four collect a selection of advertisements which represent all the types mentioned in the list above. Discuss within your group the merits of those you have collected. Can you determine the target audience they are meant for? It is likely that the advertisements contain both words and pictures. If you hide the words can others in your class tell what the advertisement is for? If they can, is it because they recognise it? Can they remember where they saw it?

Advertising agencies

To convince us that we wish to buy a product, contribute to a charitable concern, support an action group or whatever, the message their advertisement gives us must appeal to us and produce an image that we either like or sympathise with.

It is likely that large manufacturers and retailers will employ the services of an advertising agency. The agency will have professional people who have been trained in all aspects of the advertising business. Advertising involves the expertise of writers, artists, photographers, production crews and statisticians. From these, a group will be brought together to work on each manufacturer's behalf, known as an account group. They will include:

- the **account executive** who supervises the account and liaises with the client.
- the **media buyer** who investigates and 'buys' media space or time.
- the **creative team** which consists of a copywriter and art director who create and develop drawings or illustrations and any wording. They commission the artwork and select companies to make commercials.
- the **planner** who uses market research to assess the likes/dislikes of the consumer and will decide on the best strategy for the campaign and 'tests' on consumers.
- the **TV department** which organises the 'shoot' of a commercial, oversees the editing and supplies the finished commercial.

·DATA FILE·

Advertising

Planning your advertising campaign

In a small advertising group begin to plan your own advertising campaign. You should already know what your product is, what it contains, your target market and the name of your product.

Decide on the message of your campaign. Look at the section 'The advertising company' in the *Key stage 3 core*, pages 138 and 139, which shows the type of promotion carried out for selling cars. It may offer some suggestions which you could use.

Are you planning to have a company 'logo'? Look at the examples shown. Without any wording accompanying them it is likely that you can say which companies they represent. A strong company logo is one which has become very familiar to the consumer. Because of past experience of frequently seeing these logos they become familiar and therefore effective advertising for the company. This is also an example of 'silent' advertising because we recognise them without supporting words, jingles or phrases.

Would a catchy 'jingle' be a good way to promote your product? We memorise these without realising. They are another way of making products familiar. Do you know:

' .... helps you work, rest and play'?

' once ...., forever smitten'?

' the .... with the hole'?

Making up jingles can be fun but it is not easy. Have a go!

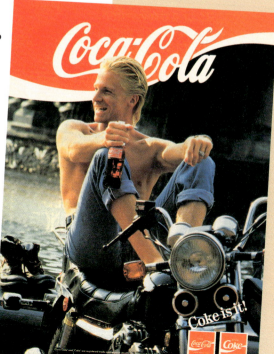

'Saving it', pages 60 and 61, in the *Key stage 3 core* may help you with your planning for launching your new product. It deals with the way in which a store could generate the interest of its customers in purchasing 'organic vegetables'.

Conclusion

It is important to a company that they monitor not only the success in sales of a 'new' product but also ensure the quality is constant. Working as a team, store staff, Environmental Health Officers (employed by the local authority), technologists and quality assurance keep a check on goods throughout their shelf-life. They will monitor storing temperature and physical/chemical conditions. Technical staff will purchase products from stores and send them to the company laboratories for checking for quality. Tesco test 500 items in this manner every week at their laboratories. Any unsatisfactory results are reported to the supplier immediately. All this is done on a basis of weekly reports to ensure the product on offer is constant and of good quality.

Having fully developed your product and planned its promotion in the fullest sense you may now think of increasing the quantity you produce. This will involve looking at the possibility of running a large-scale production line for the product you are making. The following chapters of this book will help you plan this.

▲ *This three-part lorry, which takes food to stores, has three storage temperatures, 1 frozen, 2 cool and 3 ambient.*

IS IT A system?

In design and technology we are often involved in designing systems. However it is not easy to define exactly what is meant by 'system'.

Some definitions are:

- 'a set of connected things or parts' (Pocket Oxford Dictionary)
- 'a set of objects or activities which together perform a task' (National Curriculum)
- 'a set of building blocks, which work together to produce a more complex whole, which itself does something' (glossary of the STEP Key Stage 3 core)
- 'A system is a set of interactions best described in flow-block diagram form' (STEP)

- A thorough way to define a system is a four-point description. All four points have to apply if what you are using can be considered a system:

'(1) The system is made up of parts or activities which do something.

(2) The parts or activities are connected together in an organised way.

(3) The parts or activities affect what is going through the system so that it is changed when it leaves the system.

(4) The whole thing has been identified by humans as of interest.' (Open University)

A system can be described by a flow-block diagram or an influence diagram.

Flow-block diagrams

These diagrams usually show very little detail. They are used to give an overview of a large, and often complex, process and allow designers to design a system without getting too involved in the detail. Each block, or **sub-system**, contains a word or words which may describe a quite complex series of operations. Flow-block diagrams show how major aspects of a system link up and how materials or information pass from one part to another.

Flow-block diagram showing the system for feeding a family

Influence diagrams

These show how parts of a system affect other parts. They can be useful tools in helping to think about situations or problems. You may be able to suggest other links or even more headings for this diagram.

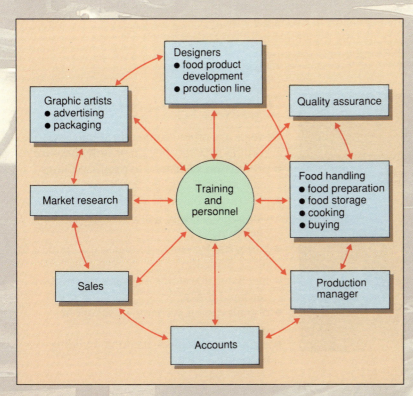

Influence diagram showing how groups or people involved in food production might influence each other

Some common *pitfalls*

There are some situations where you might think you are using a system when it is just a **simple procedure**. These situations are best described with sequence diagrams and flow charts.

Sequence diagrams are used to show the order of an operation, often without the use of words, such as how to put together a toy or model.

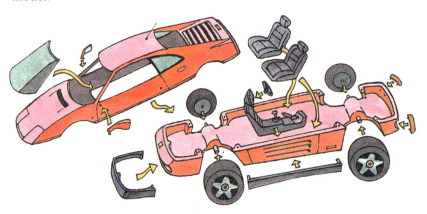

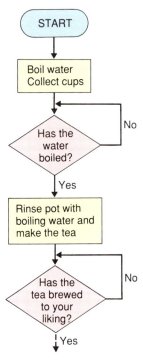

START

↓

Boil water
Collect cups

↓

Has the water boiled? — No

Yes ↓

Rinse pot with boiling water and make the tea

↓

Has the tea brewed to your liking? — No

Yes ↓

Flow charts show the stages of an operation using words to summarise what is happening. For example, when doing a flow chart to make a cup of tea, one of the instructions might be 'boil water'. This really means 'fill the kettle with water, plug it in, switch on and wait until it boils'.

Flow charts are ideal to show when a decision has to made which will affect what happens next. They are usually drawn using symbols recommended by the British Standards Institution.

·D A T A   F I L E·
Systems: introduction
Control systems: introduction

Types *of systems*

Systems are often grouped in some way according to what they do or how they work:

● production systems – to produce things such as food, clothes, toys etc;
● electronic/computer systems – to work a camera, computer game or supermarket checkout;
● biological systems – to digest our food or to make penicillin;
● mechanical systems – sewing machine or car hand brake;
● organisational systems – a school or business;
● economic systems – banking, building societies.

Some common features of systems

Sometimes you will see systems shown in a diagram form like this. This is a simple one showing the workings of a chocolate factory.

The next diagram shows the same thing, only in more detail.

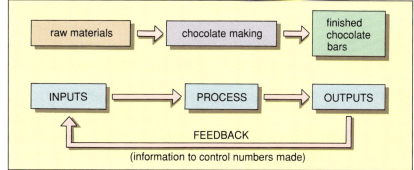

raw materials → chocolate making → finished chocolate bars

INPUTS → PROCESS → OUTPUTS

FEEDBACK

(information to control numbers made)

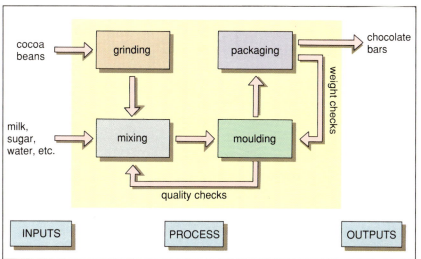

Terminology

The basic terms which are used in system design are input, process, output and feedback.

INPUT

This is information, materials, or energy which is passed into the system.

PROCESS

This is what happens to the information, materials or signal as it goes through the system; it is usually changed in some way.

OUTPUT

This is what the system does, or the changes that the system brings about.

FEEDBACK

This is some part of the output which affects the inputs. Feedback can act in one of two ways: positive or negative feedback.

Negative feedback controls the input in order to keep the output stable. For instance, in the case of *Whizzer* bar production, if the warehouse was getting full the wholesaler would tell the factory to send fewer boxes of bars. However, if stocks in the warehouse were getting low, the wholesaler would ask for more boxes. This should tend to keep the warehouse well stocked with *Whizzer* bars.

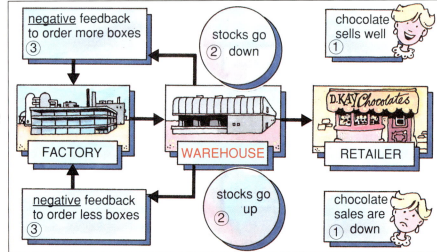

In **positive feedback** an increase in the output promotes an increase in the input. For example, if a company began making a new chocolate bar, at first the high total costs of making a few bars would mean that the cost of each bar would need to be high. As promotion and advertising increases sales, more bars would be made so the cost of making each bar would decrease. Then the bars could be sold at a lower price which would encourage more people to buy. So feedback from increased sales would eventually cause further increased sales.

Positive feedback is not common because it causes the system to become unstable. Eventually other feedbacks, which are negative, usually take effect to bring stability to the system.

·D A T A F I L E·
Control systems: introduction
Electronic systems

Other terms *used in systems*

LAG

This is the time it takes for the system to respond to a change.

Suppose the chocolate factory found that *Whizzer* bars started to sell really well. The shops would be the first to know that the demand for the new chocolate product had gone up. They would tell the wholesaler that they wanted another delivery. The wholesaler would tell the factory to send more boxes. The factory, in turn, would have to step up production of bars. This time delay between increased demand and satisfying that demand is called the lag.

STABILITY

A stable system is one that is not easily changed or upset. If it is changed then it returns to normal (within certain limits) quite quickly. In our example a stable system will keep the stocks of *Whizzer* bars at the warehouse at reasonable levels.

BOUNDARY AND SUB-SYSTEM

This is an imaginary line which can be drawn around some part of the system so that it can be considered separately from other parts as a sub-system. The system designer then only has to consider the inputs and outputs from the sub-system without having to be concerned (at least at first) with the details of what happens in the sub-system. In the example of the flow-block diagram on page 63, each block of Grinding, Mixing, Moulding and Packaging is a separate sub-system.

What's happening?

Try doing a flow-block diagram of one or two of the following examples. In each case be specific about what is flowing, most often it is some material.

- The signals which pass in and out of a television
- What happens to food in the digestive system
- An electronic burglar alarm
- A factory production line to make Christmas decorations

Designers often start by producing a top level system design which describes how the whole system will work, how it is formed from sub-systems and how the outputs from sub-systems will form inputs to other sub-systems. They can then concentrate their efforts on each sub-system because, if they can make each one work as required, then the whole system should come together successfully.

A possible stock control system in a supermarket

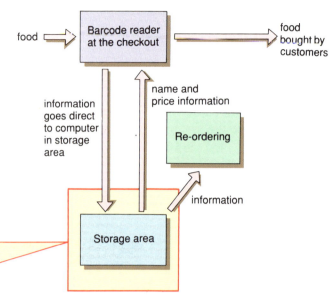

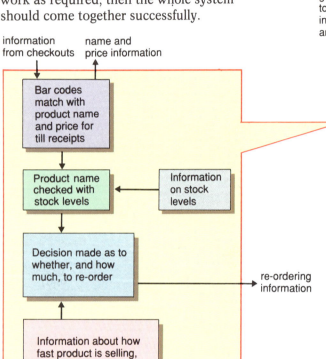

Making your own system diagrams

When you are designing a system it is important to remember that the systems approach is intended to make it easier to design and understand a particular process or situation. The diagram you use is only a tool to help you to understand and design the system and to explain your ideas to others. You can make up your own mind where to draw in boundaries which will be helpful.

Also, there is no definitive rule about how to identify a sub-system. A supermarket store could be thought of as a complete system in itself, with its own sub-systems, or as a sub-system of a whole chain of stores.

Questions to try on the chocolate production systems at Cadbury's

Look at the picture of a man putting *Crunchie* bars into boxes.
- What inputs are shown here?
- What outputs are there?
- From the picture, can you say what would happen if the man could not keep up with how fast the bars were moving along the conveyor belt? What systems term would you use to describe this?

In the next picture you can see a lady checking the operation of a machine that wraps up *Wispa* bars.
- What are the inputs to the machine?
- What are the outputs from the machine?
- In what ways can the lady control the system to make sure that it is stable and keeps working?

In the third picture you can see boxes of *Biarritz* coming off the production line. A number of things now happen to the the boxes of *Biarritz* chocolates. For example:
- the weight of each box is checked to see that it falls within an acceptably narrow range,
- the boxes are packed together in cartons for shipment,
- the pallets are moved to the factory warehouse,
- the pallets are loaded onto the lorries,
- the lorries take the chocolates to the four national distribution centres,
- lorries take the boxes of chocolates to shops as they are needed.

- Draw a diagram to describe what happens to the *Biarritz* boxes.
- Which of the types of diagrams we have been looking at in this section is most appropriate?
- At which points do you think there needs to be some feedback?
- How would you show the feedback on the diagram?

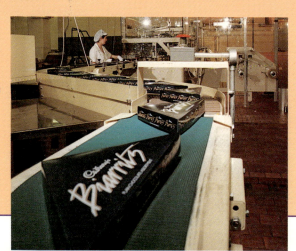

DESIGNING YOUR OWN FOOD PRODUCTION SYSTEM

In this section you will be able to design a working system for producing a food item in quantity. Many of the features of systems discussed in the last chapter should form part of your design.

There are two approaches to this project that you could follow, with lots of possibilities for individual or group design tasks within each.

- **The food approach**
  This looks at how to set up a real food production system and at how to make it a success in business terms. You could use this approach when making food for a school function or as a mini-enterprise activity.

- **The working model approach**
  This approach follows the designing and making of a working model of the food production line, and includes ways of controlling what happens on the line so that the system works efficiently. This is covered on pages 81–7.

In either approach, before you start, you will need a clear overall idea of what you want your system to do. You will need to write a design task and specification. The **design task** simply states what you are trying to do. A **specification** is more developed and sets criteria for success. These criteria can be compared with actual results at the end of the project to decide if you have produced a good design.

A word about safety!

If you decide to produce food for other people to eat, and especially if you intend to sell the food, make sure you know what the safety requirements are. Companies have to meet very strict health and safety regulations, and quite rightly so. Your teacher may decide that producing food for sale is unwise and that it is better for you to concentrate on producing food for your class only.

Whatever is decided, you will need to ensure that you follow all the correct hygiene procedures for yourself and for storing and handling food, and ensure that all working surfaces, tools and utensils are cleaned thoroughly.

From just **one to many**

Designing things for batch production is not the same as where only one or two things are to be made. You have to design both the food product and the system to produce it. It is no good, for example, choosing a food product that is so complicated to make that it is impossible to make enough in the time available. You must also think about the situation that you are designing for and the preferences of the customers. Some suitable ideas for this project are scones, pizzas, salad snacks, biscuits, chocolates, high energy bars, sandwiches and savoury dips.

When choosing the food to make you will need to take into account all the sound principles of good product development given in 'Developing a food product', page 28. If you have a good product you will need to start thinking about designing the system to produce a whole batch. The system will need to be efficient and give you high-quality products that will appeal to your customers.

Design problems in a **batch production system**

- **Costs** – for ingredients, energy, loans for raw materials, pricing and so on.
- **Sourcing** - purchasing goods from one supplier or source. This can be less costly, less time consuming and more convenient.
- **Time** – to prepare and clean up the working area, to make, to cook, to train people and so on.
- **Product appeal** – Market research may be needed before spending money.
- **Number** – What is the target number for the production run? What happens if demand is higher or lower than expected?
- **Production facilities** – What are available and are they suitable? Do you need special facilities that have to be designed, such as a production line?
- **Planning** – Batch production requires careful planning. Do you need to do a flow chart or time plan to plan what has to be done and when?
- **Management** – If you have a team with people doing different jobs or roles, do all team members understand what they have to do? Have they been briefed about it? What happens if someone is away? What happens if there is a dispute? How do you ensure that the production line works well?
- **Quality assurance** – You need to make checks throughout the production process so that the quality of the ingredients and the products is kept up to standard and that portion size stays the same. What do you mean by 'up to standard'? What will happen if the products are not of the required standard?
- **Quality control** – Checks also need to be made at the end of the production process, such as checks on weight and food quality. What will be your standard and how will you deal with the rejects?

Designing the system – **where to start?**

You could start by setting up a 'company', that is getting together a team to represent a small business. You will need to decide how large your team will have to be. Your class may be large enough for there to be two or three teams (or competing companies) working independently. Each team would be responsible for the design of the whole production system.

Within each team you could have individuals taking on the roles of people involved in the production process. It is not essential that you select roles that precisely match those used commercially, but you should think carefully about the roles you will need. The list opposite gives ideas about the responsibilities of the different roles. You may also need some people to take on more than one area of responsibility. Each of the smaller groups should meet at intervals to explain their ideas to each other and the rest of the team and to share thoughts about making improvements.

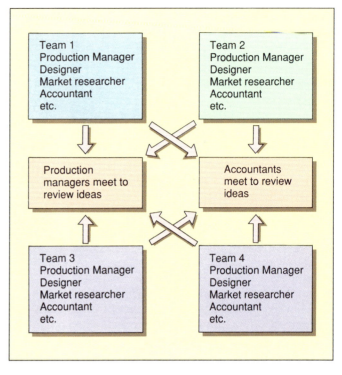

Team 1
Production Manager
Designer
Market researcher
Accountant
etc.

Team 2
Production Manager
Designer
Market researcher
Accountant
etc.

Production managers meet to review ideas

Accountants meet to review ideas

Team 3
Production Manager
Designer
Market researcher
Accountant
etc.

Team 4
Production Manager
Designer
Market researcher
Accountant
etc.

If you have several design teams in the class, when you reach the production stage, members of other teams could act as your production line workers and vice versa. It is always fun to see how others people's ideas work out in practice, but remember that you will be in the same position when it is their turn!

It might help if everyone has a **job description** which members of the team agree is reasonable. The list opposite will give you some idea about the types of task each job involves. You may want to discuss and agree on the details according to the strengths and interests of the people in your team.

It is important that each group decides on the exact design task and specification it is working to. There is more information on page 82 to help you with this.

- **Managing Director** – oversees the operation of the whole company; meets with other managers; organises jobs and responsibilities of employees; has ultimate responsibility for major decisions which affect the company.
- **Production Manager** – is responsible for all aspects of producing the goods, including stock control, quality control and the efficiency of the daily running of the production. Might also be responsible for the layout of the working area and that food and equipment are handled properly and hygienically.

- **Accountants** – sort out the business aspects of the project, such as costing, pricing, working out the break-even point, keeping a budget and generally keep an eye on all financial aspects of the work.
- **Designers** – produce ideas for company name and logo and prepare suitable advertising for the products.
- **Stock control** – make sure production line is never allowed to run out of essential materials, and that nothing is wasted. May come under responsibility of the Production Manager.
- **Production line designers** – design how the production line will work and how all the associated activities fit in (see diagram on page 75).

- **Quality assurance** – involves ensuring that all aspects of the production process are checked to ensure top quality products. Would be under responsibility of Production Manager.
- **Market Researcher** – carries out market research to make sure that there is a real need for the product, and that advertising is working well.
- **Sales force** – sell the product. May have a Sales Manager to train and coordinate their work.

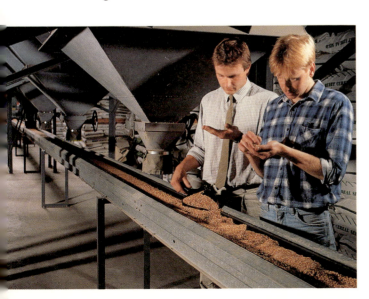

Does it **work?**

When your design team think that they have worked out enough of the details to make a trial run worthwhile, have a go! Then you will see where the problems lie and where changes are needed. If you intend to use real food eventually, then it is important to model the production system first so that you do not waste the food.

To model a conveyor belt system you could use a long piece of computer paper and loop it around some tables to make a conveyor belt that can be gently moved along by someone. You could set up work stations along the production line and have quality assurance points, such as a weighing station to ensure that each portion is correctly weighed out.

In the first run through, you could model the food using LEGO bricks, coloured paper, plasticine or whatever you think might be similar to the real thing. Try timing each small operation and look for bottlenecks in the production that slow it up.

Questions to think about when **designing your food production system**

- Are there any hold-ups in the production line which cause some people to stop work?
- Is there anyone on the production line who has too much to do to keep up?
- Can one person do what two people are doing at the moment?
- Is there a production manager to oversee the whole system?
- Have you timed how long it takes to make a certain number of the product? Can you reduce this time?

·D A T A   F I L E·
Food: storage
Presentation of ideas:
introduction
Making a time plan

- Do the managers discuss ideas and listen to the views of others or just impose their own ideas?
- How do you choose people for the job?
- Does everyone have a job description?
- Is everyone having a fair share of all the jobs?
- Have you considered swapping jobs to give others a chance?
- Are you going to have a product launch? If so, who is to prepare for it?
- Have you made sure that there are enough starting materials and thought about what to do with left-overs (stock control)?
- Should you be thinking about more than one product?
- Can you create a new market for the product?

Your trial run should allow you to produce a flow-block diagram. This would help the team to think about what happens, and in what order, on the production line, and the expected times for each part of the process.

Some flow-block diagrams, such as this one, can easily become very complicated. If this happens with yours you might find that using a simpler flow-block diagram would be better. This will not show as much detail but should still help you to design the system. It will allow you to see more clearly how the major

Production line →

	TYPE 1	TYPE 2	TYPE 3	Add cheese to all pizzas
Spoon on tomatoes and onions mixed to all pizzas	Add sweetcorn and ham	Add ham	Add ham red/green peppers sweetcorn	Add anchovies and olives to Type 2 pizzas

Heat onions and tomatoes in pan

Cut up ham

Dice peppers

Grate cheese

Peel and chop onions

Cut dough into small pizza bases

Roll out dough

Add olive oil, salt and water

Mix dough

Weigh out plain flour

Washing up!!!

Sales

Move to finished food area

Cooking

Oil baking trays

building blocks of the system relate to each other. Each of the blocks on this diagram could be expanded to show more detail, if this helps your planning.

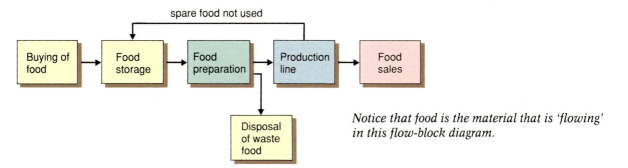

spare food not used

Buying of food → Food storage → Food preparation → Production line → Food sales

Disposal of waste food

Notice that food is the material that is 'flowing' in this flow-block diagram.

Getting down to **business**

The business aspects of a project like this might involve working out the costs, deciding on a price for the product, looking at ways of increasing profits, preparing budgets and business plans and any special sales promotions, such as '3 for the price of 2' or '20p off next purchase'.

There are two main types of costs: fixed and variable. **Fixed costs** are regular and do not change with the number made, such as costs of loans, heating, lighting, rates and so on.
Variable costs increase as you make more of your product, such as costs of food materials and packaging.

A budget sheet will help you to record the costs and revenue. The *Datafile* has other examples which you could use. Budgets are a way of setting targets for a business, that is the 'expected' figures which can be compared with the 'actual' figures at the end of the project to see how successful it was.

	BUDGET	ACTUAL
INCOME Sales of biscuits at 5p each	80 × 5p= £4.00 (estimate of numbers you expect to sell)	60 × 5p= £3.50 (actual numbers sold)
TOTAL REVENUE	£4.00	£3.50
VARIABLE COSTS Cost of materials, packaging etc.	£2.40	£2.40
TOTAL VARIABLE COSTS (A)	£2.40	£2.40
FIXED COSTS Advertising	nil	nil
Telephone	£0.30	£0.30
Heating	£1.00	£1.00
Lighting	£0.50	£0.50
Transport	nil	nil
Rent/hire of rooms	£0.70	£0.70
Gas etc.	£0.50	£0.50
TOTAL FIXED COSTS (B)	£3.00	£3.00
TOTAL REVENUE	£4.00	£3.50
TOTAL COSTS (A+B)	£5.40	£5.40
PROFIT or LOSS	– £1.40	– £1.90

In this example we make a batch of 80 biscuits but only sell 60

Since we made the biscuits in batches of 80 there is no saving on costs in having only sold 60 of the 80 biscuits made

Revenue is sometimes called income

Subtract the total costs from the total revenue to give the profit or loss

This table is one way in which you can record the information on revenue (income) and costs. The numbers used are taken from the tables on pages 77 and 79. You might prefer to use a spreadsheet instead of a table like this as it is easier to change the figures and work out the new totals. By adding more columns you could produce a budget sheet to give you a month-by-month view.

	A	B	C	D
1				
2	VARIABLE COSTS (These costs		FIXED COSTS (These costs are	
3	increase with the number made)		regular and usually do not	
4	1. Materials for cookie mix.		change with the number made)	
5	(enough to make 80 biscuits)			
6			advertising materials	nil
7	350g plain flour	£0.23	telephone	£0.30
8	2 × 5ml spoon baking powder	£0.04	heating	£1.00
9	1 × 5ml spoon salt	£0.02	lighting	£0.50
10	2 × 5ml spoon cinnamon	£0.03	transport costs	nil
11	150g soft light brown sugar	£0.27	hire of school room	£0.70
12	150g granulated sugar	£0.28	gas	£0.50
13	175g butter	£0.17	accountant's fees	nil
14	175g margarine	£0.21		
15	225g porridge oats	£0.30		
16	175g raisins	£0.24		
17	4 eggs	£0.36		
18	8 × 15ml spoon milk	£0.07		
19	4 × 5ml spoon vanilla extract	£0.18		
20	Total materials	£2.40	TOTAL FIXED COSTS	£3.00
21		sum of B7 to B19		sum of D6 to D13
22				
23				
24	2. Packaging	£0.00		
25				
26	TOTAL VARIABLE COSTS	£2.40		
27		sum of B20+B24		
28				
29	TOTAL VARIABLE COST	£2.40/80 = 0.03		
30	OF EACH BISCUIT			

As an example, in the pages that follow, we have taken the design of a production system for oatmeal cookies. Here we only look at the business aspects of the system, but if you would like to make the recipe given on the spreadsheet, your teacher will be able to give you instructions.

Spreadsheets **to the rescue**

If you have access to a computer spreadsheets are a powerful way to organise the financial aspects of the project. It allows you to model the costs in such a way that you can see at a glance the effect of, for example, an increase in the cost of raw materials or the effect of a price increase on profits.

·DATA FILE·

Information systems: spreadsheets
Cashflow forecasts and budgets

When business **is booming**

What are the effects on costs of selling more biscuits?

In this example the variable costs of making 80 biscuits were £2.40 and the fixed costs were £3.00, then the total cost of producing 80 biscuits would be £5.40.

The cost per biscuit is then

$$\frac{£5.40}{80} = £\,0.07 \text{ (rounded up)}$$

If we made 160 biscuits at twice the variable costs (£4.80) plus the fixed costs (£3.00),

the cost per biscuit would be

$$\frac{£7.80}{160} = £0.05 \text{ (rounded up)}.$$

So making more biscuits brings the costs down for each biscuit made. If you have an efficient production line you can make more of the product and so reduce the cost of making each one.

The price **is right**

You could fix any price for your product that you choose. However, there are certain things to bear in mind, for example:

- what is it actually costing to make the product?
- what would people be prepared to pay?
- how much do other similar products cost?

Your market researcher could do a questionnaire, which, among other things, would tell you what people were prepared to pay. Let's say you found out that people were prepared to pay £0.05 for each biscuit. You can then find out if you are making and selling enough biscuits to cover costs and, hopefully, make a profit. You do this by working out the **break-even point**.

A worthwhile **venture?**

If we know the fixed costs and variable costs, and have decided on the price, we can work out how many we *have* to make in order to break even. If we sell more than this number then we are making **profit**.

Assuming a price of 5p per biscuit					
SALES (number of biscuits)	0	80	160	240	320
FIXED COSTS	£3.00	£3.00	£3.00	£3.00	
VARIABLE COSTS	£0.00	£2.40	£4.80	£7.20	
TOTAL COSTS	£3.00	£5.40	£7.80	£10.20	
REVENUE	£0.00	£4.00	£8.00	£12.00	
PROFIT/LOSS	−3.00	−1.40	£0.20	£1.80	

First we make up a table like the one shown on the spreadsheet above. Note that this one uses the values of total variable and fixed costs from the previous spreadsheet. The last column of this spreadsheet is left empty for you to try out. The following notes may help you.

- **Sales** This is the number of biscuits sold; we assume that complete batches of 80 are sold.
- **Fixed costs** Put in the total fixed costs from the spreadsheet. This figure should stay the same in each column.
- **Variable costs** In our example the variable cost for each biscuit was £0.03. For 80 biscuits the total variable costs are £0.03 × 80 = £2.40. For 160 biscuits this would be £0.03 × 160 = £4.80, and so on.
- **Total costs** Add together the variable costs and fixed costs in each column.
- **Revenue** Multiply the price of the biscuit by the number made. (Assume that they are all sold.)

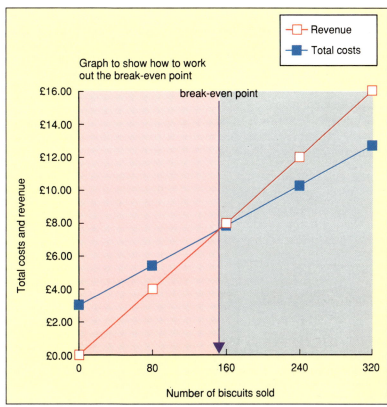

Graph to show how to work out the break-even point

- **Profit/loss** Subtract total costs from the total revenue. If the answer is a negative figure you have made a **loss**, if it is a positive figure you have made a **profit**. Where it is zero is the **break-even point**. You can see from the table that none of the columns gives a zero number for profit or loss. To find the exact point you would have to plot the lines of the total costs and revenue against batch size on a graph. Where the costs and revenue lines cross is the break-even point.

Making **more profits**

If you want your business venture to be a success you must see where you can make more profits. Look at all of the decisions you have made and re-evaluate them. If you have worked out all your figures on a spreadsheet you can now try changing some of the figures to answer some of the following questions.

- *Can you reduce costs?* Reduce the cost of one or two materials to see how it affects the total variable costs, the variable cost of each biscuit, the total costs (variable plus fixed) and the break-even point.
- *Have the number of sales been over- or under-estimated?* What happens to the profit if you don't sell all the biscuits you make, such as make 160 but only sell 100? What happens if you make and sell even larger batches?
- *Does reducing the fixed costs make much difference to the profit made?*
- *Can the price be increased?* How will this affect the profits? What problems could increasing the price cause?

Other ways to increase profits might be by:
- reducing the price to make it even more attractive. What effect will this have on the break-even point? Why could this be a high-risk approach?
- improving sales techniques or advertising.
- improving market research. Could advertising target a wider group or the product be changed slightly to give it greater appeal?

All of these will have effects on costs, such as increasing advertising or market research costs, and therefore on profits.

Finally, you will always need to know what the competition is doing. If there is a new product on the market in direct competition with yours, how will you keep up your sales?

The working **model approach**

An alternative approach to this project could be the designing of a working model, such as a conveyor belt system for part of a food production system. You could include some electronic sensing and control, and perhaps some simple pneumatics to move items off the belt for collection. You might also choose to use some computer control.

The *Datafile* contains some ideas which will help you here, and *What a Performance* looks at aspects of electronics, pneumatics and computer control.

Before you start you need to have a clear overall idea of what you want the system to do, that is you will need to write a design task or specification. On the next page are examples you could use, or you could write your own.

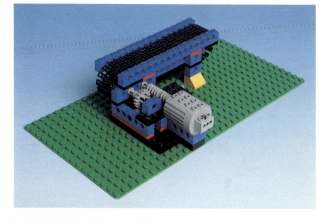

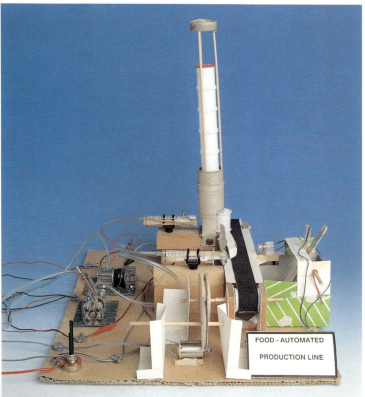

In this computer-controlled model, cotton reels are pushed onto the conveyor and a counted number of them are pushed into a collection box.

Can you work out from the picture how it is controlled?

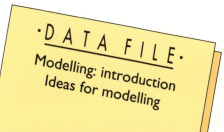

·D A T A F I L E·
Modelling: introduction
Ideas for modelling

Design task: **Putting the topping on each biscuit**

There is a problem in that the machine which puts the topping onto the biscuit works all the time even if a biscuit is not present on the line. The result is a mess which takes time to clean up and so slows down the whole production line!

Add this section to the design task if you want to make it harder.

There is also a person sitting on the line whose job it is to spot biscuits which do not have the topping and remove them. If this could be automated it would be a great improvement in quality control.

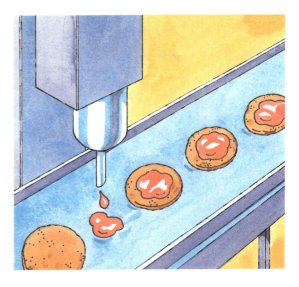

Specification: **Topping should only go on biscuits**

The motor should work each time a biscuit is present and only when a biscuit is present. The system should work automatically without the need for an operator to be present.

Add this section to the specification if you want to make it harder.

The biscuits which do not have a topping should be removed from the conveyor automatically. All this should happen with a success rate of at least 9 in 10. (You or your teacher might want to change this example to make it suit your situation more closely.)

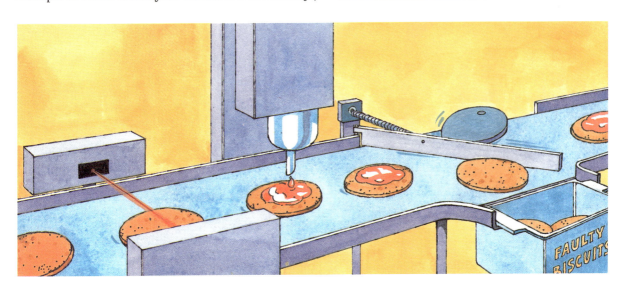

Modelling **ideas**

You could work in a design team with team members taking responsibility for specific aspects of the design, such as the conveyor belt, sensing if a biscuit is present on the line, ways of removing biscuits from the line automatically or ways of putting the topping on the biscuits. If you use computer control you will need someone to write the computer control procedures. Alternatively you could use a systems electronics kit.

The conveyor belt

You could model the belt with construction kits, such as Fischertechnik, LEGO or POLYMEK. Alternatively you could make it without such kits, using resistant materials and card. Try to model the system fairly quickly and make changes if and when necessary.

You will need to tension the belt or it may slip on the wheels at either end. A simple elastic band mechanism might do, or a spring. Can you improve on these?

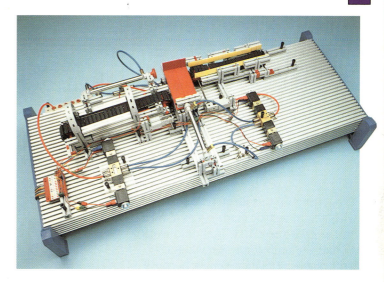

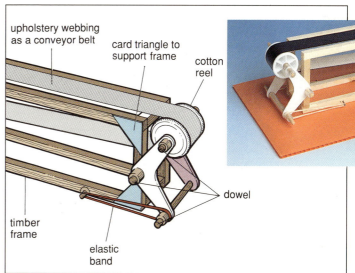

upholstery webbing as a conveyor belt

card triangle to support frame

cotton reel

timber frame

elastic band

dowel

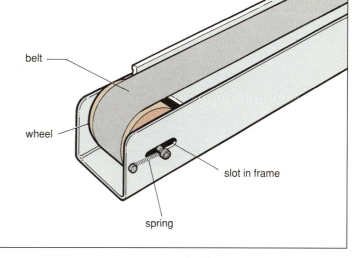

belt

wheel

slot in frame

spring

A matter of **good sense**

The following electronic systems use a light sensor, microswitch or reflective opto-switch to detect if a biscuit is coming along the conveyor belt. You could also use the reflective opto-switch to sense if the biscuit has been coated or not.

Light sensor

Try setting up this electronic system with a light sensor made up as shown on *Datafile* sheet 101. It should work so that the bulb comes on when less light reaches the light sensor because the biscuit will shield the sensor from the light source. (Think about where the light source and sensor should be positioned to work best.) The output to the system could be a motor which causes the biscuit to be coated.

Reverse leads 1 and 2 and see what happens.

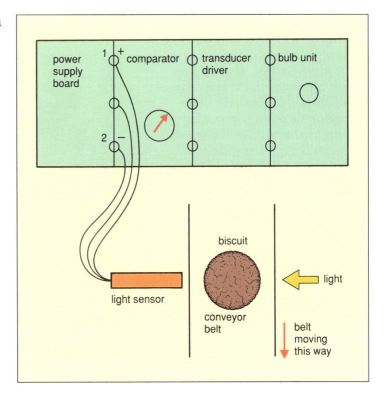

Microswitch

As the biscuits move along the belt, they could push against a microswitch. This would connect the normally open (no) terminal to the common terminal so that the current will flow and the motor will be switched on to pump topping onto the biscuit. Alternatively, the output from the microswitch could be used as an input to an interface to set a computer control procedure running.

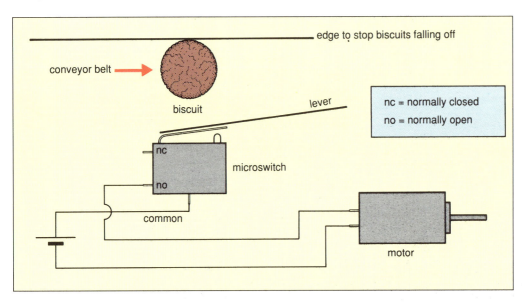

Reflective opto-switch

This sends out a tiny beam of infra-red light from one window and detects the reflection of the light in the other window if it is connected the right way round. If an object passes in front, at a distance of about 5 mm, the beam is reflected which changes the signal sent from the switch to the comparator. The comparator compares the signal from the switch with a preset value. Adjust the dial on the comparator so that the output, such as a bulb, comes on when the biscuit passes by. This should also switch on the motor to coat the biscuit. Note that we are assuming a light-coloured conveyor and a dark-coloured biscuit.

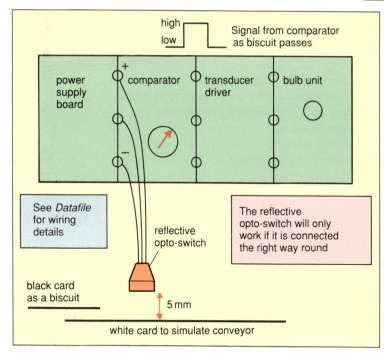

high
low

Signal from comparator as biscuit passes

power supply board | comparator | transducer driver | bulb unit

See *Datafile* for wiring details

reflective opto-switch

The reflective opto-switch will only work if it is connected the right way round

black card as a biscuit

5 mm

white card to simulate conveyor

This system can be converted to detect light-coloured biscuits on a dark conveyor by adding an inverter board into the circuit.

You could use the reflective opto-switch to detect whether the biscuit has been given its topping using the 'light on dark' and 'dark on light' systems above. Each comparator would be set to different levels to detect the difference between a coated and an uncoated biscuit. The first sensor could detect the presence of a biscuit and the second could check if it has been coated.

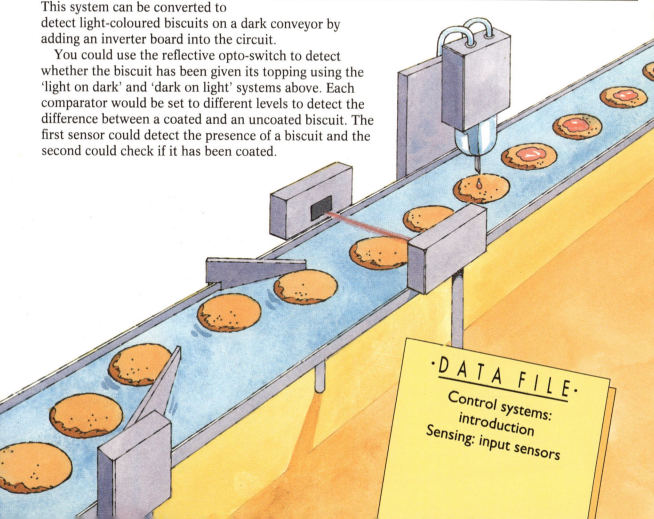

·D A T A F I L E·

Control systems: introduction
Sensing: input sensors

Jam **topping**

Here are two ideas for putting jam or butter icing onto the biscuits which are moving along a conveyor belt. They both show how to produce a steady stream of butter icing or jam. These could be modified to put a wavy line onto the biscuits.

   You will need to control the mechanism by computer or by electronic systems boards so that the jam or butter icing is only pushed out of the nozzle when a biscuit is present. Can you design a way of doing this? Make sure that the jam or icing is runny enough to be pushed through the nozzle but not so runny that it does not stay in place on the biscuit.

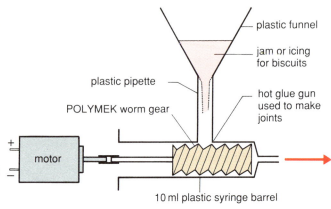

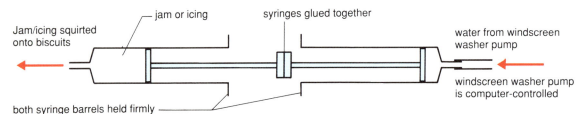

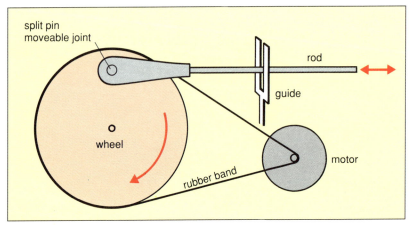

Dealing with **the rejects**

There are a number of output devices you could use to remove biscuits from the line, depending on what you have and what is suitable to your system.

- A motor could be used to push the biscuit off the line by changing the circular motion of the motor into a linear motion.
- A cam could push a flap across the conveyor and so redirect the biscuit into a container. The sensor will need to be a little way from the motor and cam so that the cam has a chance to move before the biscuit comes along.

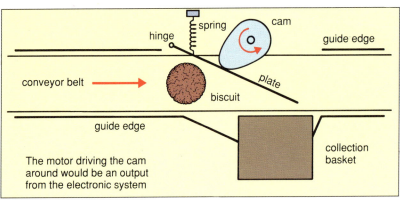

- You could use a ram-rod, which works by a small motor that moves an arm slowly out or in depending on which way round the motor is connected. It has a small clutch which slips when the arm has reached the end of its run or if it hits an obstacle which it cannot move. The clutch will wear out quickly if the motor is allowed to stay on.

  The ram-rod is best linked to a suitable lever so that the slow and quite slight movement of the arm is changed to a large movement which pushes biscuits off the line when required.

- A blast of air could be used from a pneumatic solenoid valve. The air could be directed through a nozzle giving a powerful jet of air. This could blow the biscuit off the conveyor belt. Check that the air is filtered so that it is clean.

- A pneumatic single-acting cylinder could be used to push a biscuit off the conveyor belt. The cylinder could be linked to system electronics boards so that the piston only operates when the valve receives a signal from the rest of the electronic system.

- Another pneumatic system of a syringe (without a needle) and garden spray pump could be used. The syringe barrel could be pushed out by compressed air from the spray which is pumped up prior to use. The syringe barrel could be made to return to its normal place by an elastic band.

Do not over-pump the spray. You must also only use a spray which has never been used with chemicals.

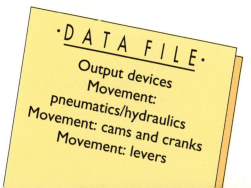

·D A T A F I L E·
Output devices
Movement:
pneumatics/hydraulics
Movement: cams and cranks
Movement: levers

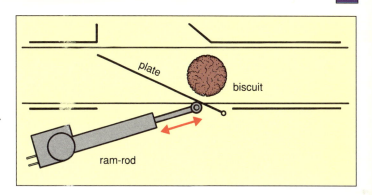

plate

biscuit

ram-rod

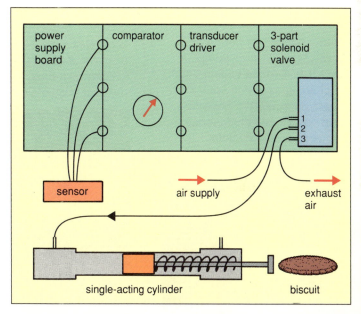

| power supply board | comparator | transducer driver | 3-part solenoid valve |

1
2
3

sensor

air supply

exhaust air

single-acting cylinder

biscuit

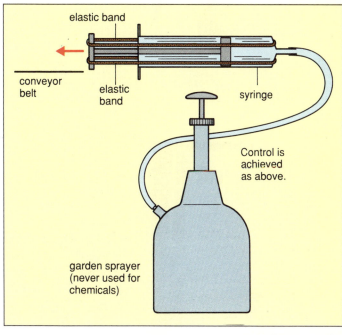

elastic band

conveyor belt

elastic band

syringe

Control is achieved as above.

garden sprayer (never used for chemicals)

BUGS beads AND BUBBLES

Biotechnology is both a new and a very old technology. In fact it is a whole collection of technologies which bring together scientific know-how and design and engineering ideas to produce useful products.

Genetically engineered seedlings growing in liquid culture medium.

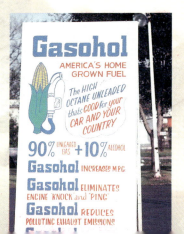

Biosystems use either living organisms, usually micro-organisms, or parts of living organisms such as enzymes to do the work. Designing a biosystem involves, among other things, providing the best possible conditions for the organisms to work in.

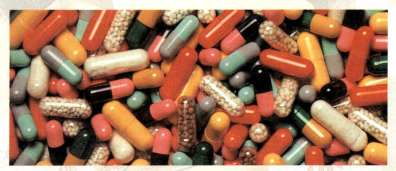

Examples of traditional biotechnology include using yeast to make breads or to ferment drinks. Cheese and yoghurt are produced using bacteria which make the essential changes to milk.

Advances in science, such as genetic engineering and cloning techniques, and the micro-electronics revolution have allowed a rapid development of the biotechnology industry. There are currently many biotechnology products which are common in everyday life, such as:

- antibiotics and many other medicines;
- sugars for soft drinks;
- sweeteners;
- foods such as bread, cheese, yoghurt, wine, beer and the microfungal food called Quorn;
- new plant varieties and tissue culture techniques for growing them;
- food thickeners, some natural food colours and flavour enhancers;
- in Brazil cars run on fuel which is a pure alcohol. In America you can buy a petrol/alcohol mixture called Gasohol. The alcohol is made from sugar cane by yeast.

See what you can find out about recent advances in biotechnology.

DESIGNING YOUR OWN BIOSYSTEM

There are many different situations and ideas for designing biosystems which you could consider. In the next few pages we look at the possibilities of these three:

● a yoghurt maker,
● a ginger beer maker,
● a hydroponics system to grow seeds.

A YOGHURT MAKER

The need

Making yoghurt on a very small scale does not need a special yoghurt maker. All you need is some pasteurised milk, a little dried milk powder and some starter culture such as a teaspoonful from a live, natural yoghurt.

If this mixture is kept warm for a few hours you will find it turns into yoghurt. The special (and harmless) bacteria in the natural yoghurt change the milk sugars into acids. These acids turn the milk proteins into the solid mass we know as yoghurt. There is also a liquid left, called whey, which is often thrown away. However, some companies are looking at ways of making good use of the whey, for example in ice cream or baby foods.

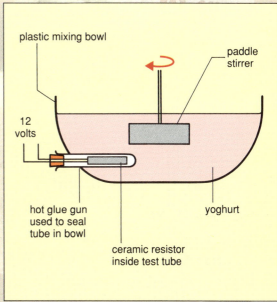

plastic mixing bowl

paddle stirrer

12 volts

hot glue gun used to seal tube in bowl

yoghurt

ceramic resistor inside test tube

The design

To make a yoghurt maker you will need a vessel which will keep the milk warm (about 25–30°C) for a few hours, possibly a way of stirring the milk, and also a way of timing the process so that you don't waste electricity once the yoghurt has been made.

You could use a systems electronics kit, a temperature sensor and a heater. Ideas for making a sensor and heater are shown on *Datafile* sheets 103 and 111. If the yoghurt will be eaten afterwards, make sure that all the equipment is cleaned thoroughly. Don't use any scientific equipment in case it has been used with chemicals. Plastic food mixing bowls or ice cream tubs make good vessels. You can also melt a hole in them with a hot glue gun to take the heater tube.

THE CONTROL SYSTEM

Your next task is to model the control system using a systems kit. Try making a system to control the temperature of your yoghurt. You could use a bulb as an output to test the system at first.

To make the output come on when the temperature is low you could either use an inverter after the comparator or reverse the sensor leads.

ALL IN A STIR

If you don't stir the mixture the yoghurt next to the heater might get too warm and the rest of the culture not warm enough. The yoghurt could be stirred only when the heater comes on. This can be done by connecting the relay to both the heater and the stirrer circuits.

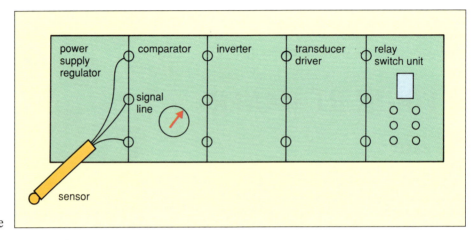

Note that the heater and motor need a higher current flow (measured in amps) than the systems kit can provide. The system controls the relay (switch) and all the power needed comes from a separate power supply.

Check that the power supply you are using can provide enough current. Your teacher will tell you how to do this.

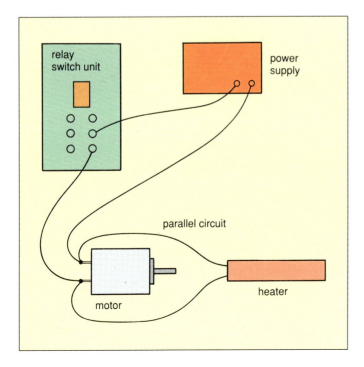

WELL TIMED

To save on electricity costs you could arrange for the heater control system to work for a few hours only to give the yoghurt a chance to set. For this you will need a pulser in your system to send pulses to a counter board. Remember that a counter, even with the pulser turned down to the slowest setting, will soon reach the end of the count. You will have to work out how to get a time period of hours. This can be done with the following boards: a pulse generator, a set of counters, a negative triggered latch, an inverter, an AND gate and the system you have made already to control the heater/stirrer. There are a number of ways of solving this problem. You must look for the best way!

TAKING IT FURTHER

If time permits you could go on to look at some or all of the following areas:

- **Making a printed circuit board (pcb) of your design.** This would give you a permanent and smaller version of the model that you created with the systems kit which could be built into your final design. Your teacher will show you how to do this.

- **Improving the yoghurt to give it greater market potential.** You could add fruit, nuts or savouries, but you will need to do some market research to find out what people prefer. You could try to think of a product which is based upon yoghurt but which is not the familiar yoghurt itself.

- **Designing cartons and packaging for the product.** This would involve labelling and perhaps advertising ideas. There are some useful software packages available which could help with the design, such as Tabs. There are also many drawing packages which can be used to create nets or developments. These have the advantage of being able to resize the drawing without redrawing it.

- **What about a mini-enterprise?** This could be a real one or a simulation. Whichever you choose, there are many business and financial aspects you will need to consider.

Accurate masks of the circuits being taped together on photo-sensitive board

The same mask can be made using a library of artwork modules put together in Autosketch and plotted out

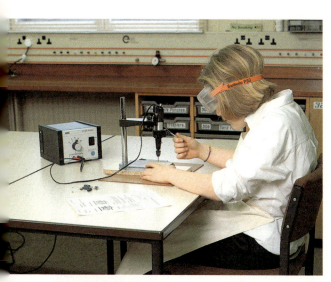

Here the etched copper-clad board is being drilled to take the components

A range of yoghurt-based products

· D A T A   F I L E ·

Electronic systems
Nets and developments
Presentation techniques
Business plans

GINGER BEER PRODUCTION

Ginger beer is a traditional drink made by a fermentation process. There are many variations on the basic recipe but they all have certain features in common. They all use yeast fed by sugars in the mixture. The yeast turns the sugars into carbon dioxide gas and a little alcohol. The gas gives the drink its fizz. The flavour is created by the use of ginger, lemons and cream of tartar. If you would like to make some, your teacher should be able to give you a recipe and instructions.

The traditional method of preparation leaves yeast in the liquid. If it was produced on larger scale there would be a problem with the yeast clouding the final product, which is not as appealing to look at.

This can be overcome by turning the process into a semi-continuous system and fixing the yeast in gel beads. The yeast is trapped in the beads but can still do its job without contaminating the ginger beer. This technique is called **immobilising** and is described fully on *Datafile* sheet 115. It is very easy to do and well worth trying. Immobilising in this way is widely used in the biotechnology industry because it does not damage the cells and reduces manufacturing costs.

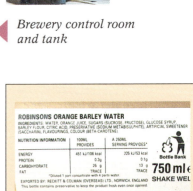

◀ *Brewery control room and tank*

Beer and lager can be made like this by using huge towers packed with baskets full of yeast beads. The wort (unfermented malt) is poured in at the top of the tower and trickles over the yeast beads. The yeast changes it to beer which comes out at the bottom.

Many other industrial processes use immobilised cells or enzymes. The sugar in some soft drinks is called fructose (fruit sugar) which is made from cornstarch using enzyme technology. This is done because fructose is 2–3 times sweeter than sucrose and so less is needed to sweeten drinks.

ROBINSONS ORANGE BARLEY WATER
INGREDIENTS: WATER, ORANGE JUICE, SUGARS (SUCROSE, FRUCTOSE), GLUCOSE SYRUP, BARLEY FLOUR, CITRIC ACID, PRESERVATIVE (SODIUM METABISULPHITE), ARTIFICIAL SWEETENER (SACCHARIN), FLAVOURINGS, COLOUR (BETA-CAROTENE).

NUTRITION INFORMATION	100ML PROVIDES	A 250ML SERVING PROVIDES*	
ENERGY	451 kJ/106 kcal	225 kJ/53 kcal	
PROTEIN	0.3g	0.1g	Bottle Bank
CARBOHYDRATE	25 g	13 g	
FAT	TRACE	TRACE	**750 ml ℮**

*Diluted 1 part concentrate with 4 parts water.
EXPORTED BY: RECKITT & COLMAN (OVERSEAS) LTD., NORWICH, ENGLAND   **SHAKE WEL**
This bottle contains preservative to keep the product fresh even once opened.

·DATA FILE·
Biosystems

A HYDROPONICS SYSTEM

Hydroponics is a way of growing plants without soil. If you give plants support and a source of mineral salts they can do without the soil. They still need water, light, warmth and air to grow.

Why might we want to design and build a hydroponics system? Here are a few ideas.
- A system for growing herbs/cress in the classroom or for the School Fayre.
- A system for growing bean sprouts to supply the local shops or supermarket.
- A system for growing fresh fodder (such as barley) for animals in the winter months.
- A self-watering plant display for a shopping precinct.
- A system for growing tomatoes that gives guaranteed results.

Hydroponic cultivation of courgettes

WHAT IS USED INSTEAD OF SOIL?

When growing seeds, such as mung beans, to produce bean sprouts there is no need to use soil because they are only grown a few days before they are eaten. All that is needed is a tray to support the seeds or a bottle to contain them. Also seeds contain all the nutrients they need for the first few days of growth, so no added nutrients are necessary.

Larger plants, like tomatoes or display plants, need support that soil usually gives. This is often done with small, very absorbent pebbles, such as Hortag. (You may have seen these underneath pot plants in garden centres.) They do not provide minerals like soil, so these will need to be added to the water.

Growing strawberry plants without soil

Hydroponic cultivation of lettuces

WATERLOGGED

Most plant roots do not like to stand in water. They need air to live in the same way as the leaves do, otherwise they get waterlogged (starved of oxygen) and rot. Since Hortag is good at soaking up water you can use pots without any base to them and supply water to the bottom of the pot. It will soak up the rest of the way. It may even be necessary to water only occasionally to avoid waterlogging roots that grow out from the bottom of the pot.

IN THE AIR

Most plants grow better in a moist atmosphere. This is best done with a spray mist system.

To make the spray you need a spray head and a way of supplying water to it. This can be done using a 12 V windscreen washer motor which will draw water up from a vessel along one tube and squirt it out along the other. For the spray head you could try blocking off some plastic tubing and making some small holes along it or using an aerosol spray head.

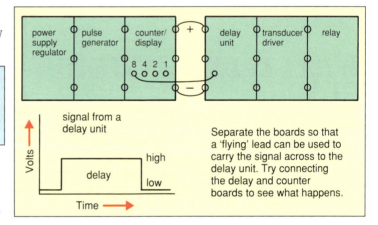

Several sprays can be driven from one pump using 'T' pieces to take off a line to another aerosol spray head.

The end of the tubing can be sealed with glue from a hot glue gun or with aquarium silicone sealer.

 Take care not to puncture the aerosol can as it will explode.

You will not need the spray to run continously, nor are windscreen motors designed to run like this, so you will need some way of switching it on and off. This would also save electricity. Can you think of a way to do this?

One way is to use a counter board with a pulser. The pulses are counted and then after a set count the output can trigger the washer motor. The motor will need to run for a short time to give a reasonable spray which can be done using a delay unit. Most delay units will give a 'high' output signal for a period of a few seconds and then the signal will drop again as shown here.

Separate the boards so that a 'flying' lead can be used to carry the signal across to the delay unit. Try connecting the delay and counter boards to see what happens.

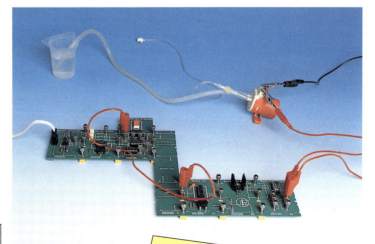

 Be careful when testing a spray system that water doesn't reach any mains electricity!

·DATA FILE·

Output devices: movement
Output devices: relays

The counter board will probably have four signal lines according to the binary counting system: 8, 4, 2, 1. These lines will be sent a signal (go high) in this order:

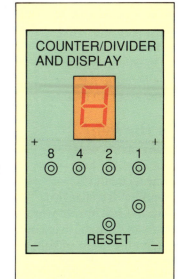

COUNTER/DIVIDER AND DISPLAY

Pulse number	Binary number			
(base 10)	(8	4	2	1)
0	0	0	0	0
1	0	0	0	1
2	0	0	1	0
3	0	0	1	1
4	0	1	0	0
5	0	1	0	1
6	0	1	1	0
7	0	1	1	1
8	1	0	0	0
9	1	0	0	1

← no trigger

If you want to trigger on a count of 9, you will need an AND gate from lines 1 and 8.

line 8 triggers on numbers 8 and 9

line 4 triggers on numbers 4, 5, 6 and 7

line 2 triggers on numbers 2, 3, 6 and 7

line 1 triggers numbers 1, 2, 5, 7 and 9

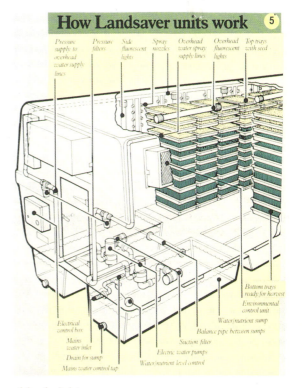

How Landsaver units work

THE BIG DRIP

One way to water seedlings efficiently would be to stack the trays they are growing in and drip water through from the top to the lower trays.

The horses in the 1984 Seoul Olympic Games were fed on fresh barley produced by a hydroponics system. It was designed to be towed as a trailer unit and had eight shelves in it. Each day a tray of seeds was put on the top shelf and all the other trays were moved down a shelf. Water was sprayed onto the top tray and filtered through to the lower trays. After eight days the seeds that went in at the top had reached the bottom and were ready to be fed to the horses. This provided a continuous supply of fresh barley.

Keeping warm

Most plants also like to be kept warm, especially in winter. The *Datafile* has some ideas on this.

In the light

Many plants need long daylight hours to grow well but the length of day changes with the seasons. In winter there may not be enough hours of daylight to encourage healthy growth. You can extend the hours of light by providing extra light of the right kind. 12 V halogen lamps are good but make sure that you use the kind that come enclosed in a reflective case as they get very hot. If the bulb is touched when cold it will probably break when it heats up.

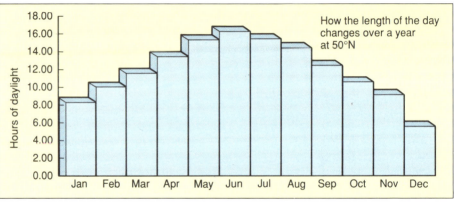

How the length of the day changes over a year at 50°N

Flashing light

Some plants are said to grow best when they are given rapidly alternating dark and light (such as 1 min dark, 1 min light). Bulbs don't last long if you switch them off and on rapidly a lot. How else might you provide alternative light?

The right time

Some plants only flower when exposed to particular hours of light and dark. Could you design a way of timing when the light should be switched on and off?

Chrysanthemums only flower after exposure to long nights and short days. This is often done artificially by growers to bring plants into bloom at different times of the year.

201552